# HOW
# TO
# SUCCEED

*DYNAMIC MIND PRINCIPLES*
*THAT TRANSFORM YOUR LIFE*

BY

BRIAN ADAMS

*Melvin Powers*
*Wilshire Book Company*

12015 Sherman Road, No. Hollywood, CA 91605

ACKNOWLEDGEMENT

The Quotation introducing each SUCCESS PRINCIPLE is reprinted from
THE NEW DICTIONARY OF THOUGHTS, 1963
J. G. Ferguson Publishing Company (Standard Book Company), New York

Library of Congress Catalog Card Number: 85-051181
ISBN 0-87980-413-0
Printed in the United States of America

*A* successful man is he who receives a great deal from his fellowmen, usually incomparably more than corresponds to his service to them. The value of a man, however, should be seen in what he gives and not in what he is able to receive.

ALBERT EINSTEIN

# The Author

Brian Adams' career reads like a page from his own book. He is an accomplished actor-writer-director. At the age of twenty-three he owned a chain of newspapers and a radio and television production company in Canada. He is an international lecturer on success and has hosted his own TV programs in Canada, America and Australia.

Born in Australia, he began his career as a copy writer for a Sydney advertising agency. Later he left on a soldier-of-fortune life that took him to many countries in the East, in Europe and to America.

After an absence of 15 years, Brian Adams was brought back to Australia by Sydney's Channel 10 to host their "Tonight" show for a year. Recently he set up BRIAD PRODUCTIONS AUSTRALIA to produce TV and film programs.

As a lecturer, he has conducted numerous seminars on 'salesmanship', the 'self image' and related success topics both in Sydney and abroad. In fact, he is considered one of the top ten motivational speakers in the United States. He has an impressive list of speaking credits which includes companies, men's and women's clubs, chambers of commerce and colleges.

Much of the lecture material is included in this book along with proven success techniques of other successful individuals.

Brian Adams knows the ingredients for health, happiness and prosperity and this book gives YOU the key for the expansion of YOUR life. At present he is working on another title—"Grow Rich with Your Million Dollar Mind".

# WHAT THIS BOOK WILL DO FOR YOU

*You are born to succeed,* anyone who tells you differently is ignorant of a universal truth. But make no mistake, success seldom arrives on a platter. It is achieved by those who adhere to universal principles—ageless laws that point the way to a richer and more satisfying life. This knowledge, or the lack of it, is the reason one individual succeeds while another fails.

HOW TO SUCCEED offers dynamic techniques to awaken dormant talents and presents numerous cosmic laws to assist you in the development of personal powers through the utilization of your mind. Armed with this knowledge, you are ready to transform your life: success for failure, health for sickness, happiness for misery.

Self-management of the mind is the key to *all* success; what you think, feel and believe, you ultimately become. To master your own destiny you must control your thought processes. Not until this is done will you be able to overcome those 'disdainful forces' that crop up continually to plague you.

Despondency, inferiority, disappointment, tension and fear are self-imposed destructive forces brought about by a pattern of negative thinking.

This *pattern* must be changed before the necessary elements which make for total living can enter your life. Affirmative and negative thought patterns cannot occupy your mind at the same time—one or the other must dominate. The pattern which consistently dominates decides your future: well being or mental and physical deterioration, success or failure.

HOW TO SUCCEED explains the principle of *thought pattern control*—MIND OVER ALL. To apply thought pattern control is to govern the greatest force known to man—*cosmic mind power*. It is the necessary 'key' to the demonstration of health, happiness, love, inner peace, self-confidence, material wealth—indeed the accomplishment of everything that makes life a joyful experience.

You are the president of a corporation—'SELF'. If there are present negative conditions holding you back, you alone are responsible—not others or external circumstances. It is your response to situations—what you think, feel, then ultimately do that determines the success or failure of 'SELF' . . YOU must rule. YOU must take charge of your corporate 'body' and dictate how you want it administered. If you wander through life waiting for others to hand you your 'just dues', that is exactly what you will receive . . . *Your destiny is in your own hands.*

HOW TO SUCCEED shows you how to gain a new understanding of your inner 'self' and how to develop an effective self image. It presents the laws that govern your success or failure and gives you a fresh look at life; a new-found enthusiasm for what lies ahead. This book shows you the way. It is your starting point, your guide to discovering and utilizing the high-powered forces within.

And that is what HOW TO SUCCEED is all about—*a practical guide for overcoming limitations and getting from life that which you most*

BRIAN ADAMS

8

# SUCCESS

*Think of the days you have lost to defeat.*
*They are as dead leaves on a plant. Snip them.*
*The roots are alive awaiting the water*
*from your hand that new growth will emerge,*
*for life must flow through you, not to you.*

*Remember when young how each day was adventure?*
*The sun never rose soon enough and why did it set?*
*Then one morning it rose too soon and set too late.*
*You were adult, 'grown up', but in ways regressed.*

*Each morning should find you aglow with the chance*
*of testing your courage and moving ahead*
*to that goal which may seem as far away as youth.*
*If sorrow and pain knock you down, know that*
*joy and pleasure are bought with these coins.*

*When tired and sure that life has bypassed you,*
*take another glance. It is then that wisdom,*
*sweetness of soul, and inward peace will be yours.*

*The tools for creating a masterpiece of life are here.*
*You are the artist. Success will depend on your faith.*

*And what should success look like?*

*Success is vivid, colored with bright hues*
*brought about by the power of you to rule yourself.*
*When you want friendship, it is with you.*
*When you desire love, it enwraps you.*
*When you seek wealth, it enfolds you.*

*Your masterpiece has balance and design*
*brought about by your hand which has placed*
*all that you experience in proper proportion.*
*The focal point is clear, past worries do not appear.*


*Your masterpiece has feeling, a soul that radiates*
*and harmonizes with the exterior, greater self,*
*for it is that strength which moves other men.*

*That is success. That is yours.*
*That is what you are about.*

JANE PERRY

**DEDICATED TO:**

all those whose faith and
inspiration have elevated
my own sights. There have
been many . . .

# SUCCESS PRINCIPLES

# YOU ARE BORN
# TO SUCCEED

*Success Ideas in this Chapter*

- Everyone Can Succeed
- What Success Should Mean To You
- Why One Person Fails And Another Succeeds
- Be On The Side Of Success
- You Are Not A Statistic But A Creative Individual
- To Succeed Creatively You Must Express Your True Self
- You Are Unique So Why Not Let Others See It?
- Be A Creator Not An Imitator
- The 5-POINT PLAN To Discover Hidden Talents
- You Succeed When You Think Success
- Even A Small Amount Of Faith Is Better Than No Faith
- Grow By Meeting Challenges Head On
- Man Is A Worry Wart
- Future Events Have A Habit Of Not Showing Up
- Claim Success In Everything NOW
- It's Up To You To Choose Success
- Success Is Programed Accuracy—Not Luck
- How To Program Your Life Effectively
- 5 PROGRAM IDEAS To Help You Win Success
- To Succeed Apply Common Sense Principles
- 4 Basic ACTION STEPS To Help You Succeed
- Call Upon Great Minds To Help You Succeed
- A Personal Library Is The Best Investment
- The Key To Becoming A Self Power
- Abilities You Need To Become A Self Power
- Summary Of Ideas To Help You Succeed

14

# 1

*The road to success is not to be run upon by seven-leagued boots. Step by step, little by little, bit by bit— that is the way to wealth, that is the way to wisdom, that is the way to glory. Pounds are the sons, not of pounds, but of pence.*

CHARLES BUXTON

---

**EVERYONE CAN SUCCEED.** You are born to win. You are born to experience radiant health, happiness, peace of mind, confidence and financial success. To do so is to partake of the joys of life. You are not born into this world to experience a life-time of sickness, fear, anxiety, loneliness, poverty or failure of any degree. To experience failure continually is to deny God's true purpose for you—an abundant, joyful, healthy and creative life.

To live in poverty, to experience unhappiness and poor health is to be out of harmony with life. To be prosperous, healthy and happy, is to be in tune with life. As you grow in years, so should you progress mentally, spiritually and materially. To be in a constant state of growth is the law of life; growth is God's plan for *all* things.

**WHAT SUCCESS SHOULD MEAN TO YOU.** Success is relative. It means different things to different people. To one individual it is the attainment of a vibrant personality, to another, the establishment of a fine home and happy family life, to someone else, the acquisition of vast wealth and power. What signifies success to one individual may not mean a thing to another.

However, everyone would agree that success includes the following: freedom from fear, worry, anxiety, frustration, failure and poverty; the acquisition of personal happiness, health, joy, peace of mind, love, self-respect, family accord and financial security.

15

Success is also the accomplishment of desired goals through the exploitation of creative abilities. It is the favourable termination of anything attempted. It means gaining from life that which you most desire.

**WHY ONE PERSON FAILS AND ANOTHER SUCCEEDS.** As part of my research to find out what makes people as they are and the reason one individual will fail while another succeeds, I have spent a great deal of time questioning business and professional men, psychologists, students of philosophy and religious leaders of the various denominations. From these discussions I have concluded that there is, suprisingly enough, a simple answer. The reason one individual succeeds and another fails is because the successful man knows the reason for his 'being' and uses his creative thinking powers affirmatively to create and control his destiny. The failure type individual struggles through life unaware of his true purpose on earth and fails to use—in a constructive manner—the creative powers at his command.

**BE ON THE SIDE OF SUCCESS.** To know your true inner self and to understand 'why' and 'how' your mind works and what it can achieve in your life is to be on the side of success.

Man is a spiritual being as well as a physical being. Man's outlook in the Western world is geared to physical comforts. He is inclined to ignore his spiritual being. Eastern philosophers teach that the physical body is unimportant, only the spirit occupying this temporary vehicle is eternal. Therefore, man should reflect on the purpose of his being to gain a greater understanding of himself, things around him and other people.

**YOU ARE NOT A STATISTIC BUT A CREATIVE INDIVIDUAL.** In Ancient Egypt there existed mystery schools where men of vision probed the secret of man's being. Great discoveries were made which astound us even today. The sages of ancient times knew that before man could control his destiny he had to comprehend the truth of his being. The wisdom of this thinking remains as potent and as practical in our present day society as it was several thousand years ago in Egypt.

There is a definite reason for man's being. He is not—as some people would have us believe—a mere statistic. He is not born into this world 'to exist' or to experience a lifetime of misfortune. This premise would be contrary to the natural creative forces operating throughout the universe for man's growth.

Life is a giant highway on which man is a traveller. At the beginning there is birth. Somewhere along the way there is physical death. Beyond that, the mystery of eternity. On the physical plane, man has been granted *free will*, or control of his life to do with as he wishes. In order to reap the 'fruits of life', man must become aware of his *divine purpose*; he must know *who he is, what he is* and *where he is headed*.

Man's primary purpose on the spiritual plane is to seek a closer reunion with God. Man's purpose on the mental as well as the physical plane is to discover and use the creative talents bestowed upon him by his Creator for the betterment of himself and his fellow man. God made you a creative individualist and He wants you to *succeed*—not fail.

**TO SUCCEED CREATIVELY YOU MUST EXPRESS YOUR TRUE SELF.** You have been created in the image of God, therefore, you must strive to express *perfection*, even though you are less than perfect. If you are dissatisfied with your life it is because you are failing to express your creative self; you are straying from your true purpose.

*Life within is God*. To allow this *truth* to permeate your being is to experience a sense of oneness with your Creator. You are possessed with the strength and wisdom to *change* every negative aspect that has been holding you back. *The truth will always set you free*—free of earthly limitation and lack.

Release your mind from the shackles of superstition and ignorance— *negative thinking*—which holds you from your true purpose. You are here to express all that is 'good' in a creative way. Find the level of your creative ability and express it.

**YOU ARE UNIQUE SO WHY NOT LET OTHERS SEE IT?** There is no one in this world quite like you. Although others may look like you and imitate you, no one else can do the very same things as you in exactly the same manner. You have individual thoughts which lead to individual actions. Most important of all, you have individual talents waiting to be expressed in a personal and unique way.

Today, more so than ever before, business, professional and industrial leaders are on the look-out for individuals who can express talents in a creative way. The person who stands out as an 'individualist', who knows how to effectively put his unique talents to work, is the one most sought after in this world. It's the person who is 'different' who makes the impression and walks off with the job and the acclaim.

Knowing that you are unlike the next fellow in your thoughts, actions and talents, begin to mould a definite image, so that others in a position to help you can readily see that you are 'different' and thus worthy of consideration for more important things.

**BE A CREATOR NOT AN IMITATOR.** It is important for you to understand fully that there is absolutely no one else in this world quite like you. The abilities you have and the way in which you express them cannot be created and expressed in the same way by others. They can, however, be copied. This places you in a unique situation—*you have no competitors only copiers.*

You compete with yourself in this world by throwing up barricades in the form of negative ideas and opinions about what you *can* and *cannot* do. Unless you believe in your own abilities you come off second best. You fall prey to living your life as a copiest and not as an individualist. When this happens, you miss much of what life has to offer. As a copiest you cannot be better than the person you are copying, because you are *imitating* and not creating. This places you in direct competition with the person you are copying.

People who imitate others seldom reach great heights. Those who create and produce their own ideas are the ones who succeed, who become leaders. You have a creative mind capable of producing individual thoughts and ideas and of expressing individual talents in a unique way.

Stop competing with others. *You are you.* You are dissimilar to others mentally, spiritually and physically. Strive to create, not to imitate.

**THE 5-POINT PLAN TO DISCOVER HIDDEN TALENTS.** Everyone has hidden abilities. Your job is to discover and develop them. You could be wandering through life missing out on valuable opportunities because of your failure to tap dormant talents.

Here's how to go about discovering hidden abilities with the **5-Point Plan.**

*Firstly*, devote the next thirty minutes to writing down your good and less than perfect personality traits. *Secondly*, list the things you have accomplished and the things you wish to accomplish. *Thirdly*, write a one-page biography on your life to this present day. *Fourthly*, make a list of the compliments you have received from your family and friends: pleasant smile, firm handshake, immaculate dress, tone of voice, ability to express your point of view and so on. *Fifthly*, make a list of the things at which you excel: hobbies, sports and talents. Add to this list the things at which you would like to excel.

# THE 5-POINT PLAN

1. *List your good and less than perfect personality traits.*

2. *List the things you have accomplished and the things you wish to accomplish.*

3. *Write a one-page biography on your life to this present day.*

4. *List the compliments you have received from family and friends.*

5. *List the hobbies, sports and talents at which you think you excel. Add to this list the talents at which you would like to excel.*

Now you have a composite of 'the sort of person I am' and 'the sort of person I wish to be'. Carefully analyse what you have written and you will discover that you have qualities that you never imagined yourself to possess. Exploit the qualities that appeal to others; become fully aware of what they are and get them working for you on a BIG SCALE.

**YOU SUCCEED WHEN YOU THINK SUCCESS.** Miracles will occur in your life when you use the power of your mind in an affirmative way and when you come to the realisation that the only thing that separates you from success or failure is the way you 'think', 'feel' and 'believe'. As you 'think' and 'believe' each hour of each day, you automatically plant success or failure seeds in your deeper mind. Your habitual thinking pattern nurtures these seeds to bring forth success or failure. *Think* and *feel* that you *can* and *will* succeed. *Believe it!*

You have many innate talents waiting to be developed. Discover them. Nurture them. Believe your talents are worthy of high accomplishment and you will experience it. *Belief in victory is often a battle won.*

**EVEN A SMALL AMOUNT OF FAITH IS BETTER THAN NO FAITH.** Belief is not wishful thinking. It is strong conviction — *faith.* You cannot wish yourself into a new house but you can devise an idea, a scheme, a plan of action, back it with strong belief and then expect an affirmative result. You can bring into your life material riches, better health and greater happiness by *believing* that God means you to have these things.

> 'If ye have faith as a grain of mustard seed . . .
> nothing shall be impossible unto you.'—MATT. 17:20

**GROW BY MEETING CHALLENGES HEAD ON.** You grow to greatness by meeting challenges and successfully overcoming the problems that arise from them. Take on challenges necessary for growth. Meet them face to face and determine to conquer them. Success is found when you do something about it constructively and creatively. You are not a creature of circumstance but a free agent with your destiny resting squarely on your own shoulders. Ideas must be created, goals planned and the challenges of success taken up. Persistent effort, *faith,* the application of affirmative thought principles are the scientific ways of ensuring success.

You are in business for yourself. Train your mind to accept the fact that every set-back, every step forward, is a means of growing into success. A single failure does not mean permanent failure, nor does one success mean permanent success unless you use that initial success as a stepping stone to a higher plateau and further creative accomplishment.

*Life is action*; keep moving ahead in life regardless of the seemingly insurmountable problems that may arise. You are born to win and you *can* win if you believe strongly enough in this fact.

**MAN IS A WORRY WART.** It is the nature of man to fret and worry; worry about his family, his neighbours, his job, and his future. Worrying has become a national pastime. Fortunately, this negative attitude can be changed by changing the pattern of negative thought.

Worry alters things only in a negative way. Worry breeds fear and fear is the most common reason for failure.

Worrying about 'tomorrow' is senseless; tomorrow never really comes. It is a term to denote a future time. You cannot live in the 'tomorrow', you can only live in the present — *today*. When you worry needlessly about what will happen to you tomorrow, next month or next year, you are applying brakes to your progress by cluttering up your creative thinking powers. Don't spend one moment worrying about tomorrow's problems — live today as best you can. 'Live in day-tight compartments', is the excellent advice given by Dr William Osler. Confine your thoughts to immediate problems and events, not to possible problems that may or may not occur in the future.

You cannot succeed while harbouring a fear of the future. If you must worry at all be concerned about the problems that have bearing upon your immediate life. When you worry about the success of some future project you are wasting energy. Deal only with the things that are important to you *now*. Do *one thing* at a time — *one job at one time*.

Life is a great adventure and should be appraised from this point of view completely free from fear. If you become apprehensive about 'what's to come', then you are inviting failure. 'The thing I feared has come upon me,' said Job.

**FUTURE EVENTS HAVE A HABIT OF NOT SHOWING UP.** Do not become fearful of future events. The confident, effortless way of life is best. Accept and meet challenges as they arise without becoming fearful of them. Imagine the fulfilment of your desires. See them taking place in your mind's eye. Feel confident about every undertaking. Know that you will succeed and have the utmost faith in that fact.

Live each day as it comes. 'Tomorrow' is a term of reference for a future time, therefore, worrying about some problem that may or may not be around in the future is a waste of brain power. Confront problems each day as they arise. Give no thought to negative situations that threaten you in the so-called 'tomorrow'. Future events have a habit of changing their nature and sometimes of not taking place at all. The wise man gives no concern for hazy future events, but instead, concentrates his energy on meeting the challenges as they confront him.

**CLAIM SUCCESS IN EVERYTHING NOW.** If you are waiting for success to come to you, you may be in for a very long wait. If you have convinced your subconscious mind that health, happiness and prosperity are dependent upon some future event, time or place, then you are going to be disappointed.

Everything for a successful life is here now. Peace of mind can be yours *now*. Health can be yours *now*. Prosperity can be yours *now*. Stop living in the past or attempting to live in the future. *Live in the present.* Determine that success will be yours in every way *now*, based on your own efforts and not dependent upon any future time, place, event or person.

Write the following affirmations on a card, 3 inches by 5 inches, and place the card where it can be seen throughout your work day. *Believe* that these affirmative states are yours to claim *NOW*.

I CLAIM HEALTH NOW

I CLAIM PEACE OF MIND NOW

I CLAIM JOY NOW

I CLAIM HAPPINESS NOW

I CLAIM SUCCESS NOW

IT'S UP TO YOU TO CHOOSE SUCCESS. You won't gain anything by whimpering about your present poor state of affairs. No one is particularly interested in hearing about your failures. Stir up the gift of God within—the capacity to succeed. Don't be dependent upon anyone other than *yourself* for success or you'll be disillusioned and disappointed.

You have been given the capacity to choose; choose health, choose happiness, choose to be successful in every way.

SUCCESS IS PROGRAMED ACCURACY—NOT LUCK. The fulfilment of goals must be programed with accuracy and not left to so-called 'luck'. Every person has the ability to succeed and *can* succeed by implementing an intelligently planned set of goals backed by affirmative mind principles.

To gamble with your life by hoping, wishing, dreaming of success is foolhardy. To let 'chance' rule your destiny is madness.

Too many people wander aimlessly through life dreaming of success. They speak of their 'big break', or their 'lucky number', and on such nebulous things as these, pin their hopes. These individuals invariably are disappointed, for so called 'luck' plays no part in lasting success. 'Shallow men believe in luck, wise and strong men in cause and effect,' said the American poet Ralph Waldo Emerson.

Mathematicians maintain that: 'everything is bound by law and governed by infinite intelligence'. And they are absolutely right. Life is definite. Everything has purpose and must operate according to a well organized plan if it is to function efficiently.

The life principle is always seeking an outlet. Everything moves, changes and progresses according to plan. The rotation of the universe on a perfect time schedule, the growth of vegetation, the change of seasons, are perfect examples of principle in action. There would be chaos if this cosmic plan collapsed. How then, could man possibly think that his life could be left to mere chance? It isn't, and it would be foolish of man to think otherwise.

**HOW TO PROGRAM YOUR LIFE EFFECTIVELY.** We know that we are operating in a universe that is logical and precise and that order must pervade *all* things to ensure continuous, harmonious growth.

Apply the principle of 'order' to your life from this moment on. Don't leave the accomplishment of future goals to 'chance' or you will be disappointed. Fortunes are not acquired by haphazard investments; successful operations are not carried out by unskilled 'trust-to-luck' surgeons; jet aircraft are not piloted by 'chance' methods; computers are not assembled from 'hit or miss' plans. When a marriage partner is selected it is not by a 'I hope it works' procedure. Train, bus, plane schedules are not left to 'chance'. They are *programed accurately.* The sun does not rise at midday; the moon does not shine in the afternoon. Everything that is to be successful in life must be programed with accuracy.

Commence right now to plan your life. Cease being like a rudderless ship floundering upon rough seas. Play life as you would a chess game— *skilfully.* By planning your dreams and aspirations carefully you will avoid experiencing a series of muddles, disappointments and failures.

# 5 PROGRAM IDEAS TO HELP
# YOU WIN SUCCESS

Here are five ideas to help you program your life in an orderly way.

---

**Idea 1:** PLAN—What do you want in life?

**Idea 2:** ORGANIZE—How will you go about getting it?

**Idea 3:** DECIDE—Get the facts upon which to make accurate decisions?

**Idea 4:** ATTACK—Enthusiastically put your plan into high gear.

**Idea 5:** WIN—Persist with your plan until you succeed.

---

**TO SUCCEED APPLY COMMON SENSE PRINCIPLES.** Just as there is principle operating for nature, so too is there principle operating for the existence of man. Nature's laws and human laws parallel. And they require the guidance of a definite plan. The reason for ill health, misery and failure is the inability of human beings to comprehend and use common sense principles of living.

If you desire to assemble a radio receiver it must be built according to a set principle. If you try to put it together in a haphazard fashion it won't work. That's plain common sense. It's the same with your desire to succeed. Unless you assemble the necessary ingredients for success and devise a suitable plan of action you won't succeed.

Organize your life according to a well laid-out plan. Don't be content to amble along pinning your hopes on 'luck'. Wishful thinking is not enough to ensure success. A steady effort and *belief* in a well-devised plan of action is the ultimate key to successful accomplishment.

## 4 BASIC ACTION STEPS TO HELP YOU SUCCEED

ACTION STEP 1: UNDERSCORE BOOKS. It is difficult to remember everything that happens each day; the names of all the people you meet, the places you have been to or the things you have been told or learned. Therefore, the practice of gathering knowledge and keeping it *on file* for future reference is a worthy one that will pay handsome dividends.

Within the chapters of this book are dozens of helpful ideas and suggestions for personal success. Some of them will appeal to you and you will want to make note of them for future reference. I have always used the *underscore method* when reading a reference book so that paragraphs of interest can easily be found again.

Use the underscore method while reading this book. With a coloured lead pencil, underscore ideas that appeal to you. With specific passages underscored you will be able to quickly get to the 'meat' of each chapter. Re-read *How To Succeed* many times so that the principles 'sink in' and with application, take hold of your life in an affirmative way.

ACTION STEP 2: BE A NOTE-TAKER. Obtain a notebook and jot down ideas that appeal to you. You may learn of a particular success technique from a new acquaintance or from a lecture you have attended. Write them in your book for future reference. Always keep your notebook handy for quick insertion of appealing success ideas.

ACTION STEP 3: BE A 3 x 5 CARD-CARRIER. Get a stack of cards, 3 inches by 5 inches, and write or type appealing ideas on them. Perhaps it might be a 'thought for the day' you've copied from a calendar or the newspaper. Perhaps it's something you've heard on the radio. If it has a 'message' that appeals to you, copy it and place it in your success file. Carry a different card with you each day and refer to the message on it whenever you get a free moment.

ACTION STEP 4: BUILD A SUCCESS SCRAPBOOK. Clip articles of interest that pertain to success from newspapers and magazines. Get into the habit of clipping and filing bits of useful information. Place them in a loose leaf binder. Make it your personal success scrapbook of selected thoughts, ideas and success stories about other people. Your reference book on success will serve you well as you chart the course of your own life.

CALL UPON GREAT MINDS TO HELP YOU SUCCEED. Down through the years great men have expressed their ideas and feelings and shared their wisdom and knowledge with mankind via the written word.

It is said: *books are people*. Books present the opportunity of meeting great minds of the past and present. Through a carefully planned program of reading, one is able to appreciate the wisdom of Shakespeare, the reasoning of Plato, the philosophy of Socrates, the compassion of Lincoln and the ideas of Freud on human behaviour.

Good books help you to grow intellectually. They help you to form your own ideas, thoughts and feelings about yourself, things and others. Good books help you to succeed. They are precious tools to the man who wants to get ahead. Good books are the cheapest form of education I know.

Read everything you can afford to buy. If your budget restricts the purchase of too many good books, borrow them. Get into the habit of spending at least thirty minutes of each day reading. Start with newspapers and magazines. Progress to a book that provokes thought, inspires or gives you a greater understanding of life. Finish off your reading by studying at least one verse from the Bible. In addition to teaching the things of life you ought to know and understand, the Bible acts as an excellent mental tranquillizer when negative conditions are affecting your life.

A PERSONAL LIBRARY IS THE BEST INVESTMENT. Build a personal library of books. Surround yourself with *good* books. They are the wisest investment your 'self-corporation' can make. Take pride in your library; add to it as often as you can afford. Don't let your books gather dust; read them, underscore the ideas that appeal to you and take notes.

Begin immediately to build your library and to commence a daily reading program. If unable to purchase books, make good 'use of your local library. Start reading books that interest you; light reading at first, then move to the classics when you feel you are ready. *A minute spent gaining knowledge is a minute spent wisely and productively.*

**THE KEY TO BECOMING A SELF POWER.** You are born with free will. You have the privilege of deciding for yourself which turn of the road to take. The final decision rests within the confines of your own mind as to whether you succeed or fail; no other person can succeed for you—it's a solo act. When you attempt to ride to success on someone else's ideas and efforts, you seldom get to choose the destination.

The key to becoming a self power is to know and *believe* that you have the ability to guide your life in the direction you desire; that you create and mould your own destiny by governing your thoughts.

The riches of life are all around you for the taking if you will but use your creative mechanism—conscious and subconscious mind—to harvest them. Everyone desires a life of health, happiness and prosperity, yet few succeed in experiencing those affirmative states because of false beliefs and the misuse of their thinking powers.

## ABILITIES YOU NEED TO BECOME A SELF POWER

| THE ABILITY TO: | HOW TO ACQUIRE IT: |
|---|---|
| 1. *Express* your point of view in an articulate manner. The ability to speak effectively is the mark of a leader. | *Join* a debating society or a public speaking course. Join a toastmaster, toastmistress or rostrum club. They are listed in the telephone directory. |
| 2. *Project* an effective self image. Personality wins friends and influences people. | *Study* other people. Read a book on etiquette. Develop a warm sincere smile. Like people and show it. |
| 3. *Make* effective decisions and avoid procrastination. | *Look* at the facts. Weigh the pros cons, make your decision, then stick to it. |
| 4. *Act* in a confident manner in every situation, adverse or otherwise. | *Recall* your last success. Remember the feeling of confidence it brought? Bring this same feeling to the next challenge you take on. |
| 5. *Develop* ideas, plan goals and carry them out successfully. | *Read* every newspaper, magazine and book you can lay your hands on. Use your imagination. Mix with successful people. Write down your goals and how you intend to accomplish them. |

# SUMMARY OF IDEAS TO HELP
# YOU SUCCEED

1. **You are born to win.** *Success depends upon the creative expression of your abilities and the depth and strength of your desires.*

2. *You succeed when you develop the power of BELIEF. This is not day-dreaming nor wishful thinking, but firm conviction. FAITH in your ability to succeed is essential.* **Belief in victory is often a battle won.**

3. *Don't wait for health, happiness and success. Claim health* **now.** *Claim happiness* **now.** *Claim prosperity* **now.** *Live each day as it comes and live it* **enthusiastically,** *always expecting the best.*

4. *Life is programed accuracy, not luck. Plan and organize your life. Set about your goals in an orderly fashion.*

5. *Set up a personal success file. Take notes, clip stories that pertain to success from newspapers and magazines. Use 3 ins x 5 ins cards to write down ideas that appeal to you. Underscore ideas that appeal to you in books.*

6. **You are unique.** *No other person can think and act in exactly the same manner as you. Be a creator not an imitator. Become a leader, not a copiest.*

7. *Develop personality traits and creative talents. Make a list of the type of person you wish to be.*

8. *Acquire a library of good books. Books are knowledge. You will require a great deal of knowledge to succeed.*

# HOW THE AMAZING POWER OF YOUR MIND WORKS

*Success Ideas in this Chapter*

**2**

*It is with diseases of the mind as with diseases of the body, we are half dead before we understand our disorder, and half cured when we do.*

COLTON

---

YOUR MIND IS A CREATIVE MASTERPIECE. The most complex mechanism known is the MIND. This creative masterpiece is an invisible computer of infinite power. We know something about the mind but not *what it is*. No living person can explain in exact terms what the mind is. The mind is infinite and being so, cannot be encompassed.

Down through the ages a few forward thinking individuals have exercised a greater degree of *mind power* than their fellow man and in so doing, have raised the consciousness level of all men.

Technical achievements these past one hundred years have been more spectacular than ever before. By utilizing a minor portion of an unlimited mind power potential, men of science have unearthed many of the laws governing this universe. Yet, surprisingly enough, only the surface has been scratched in numerous attempts to advance knowledge in the area of human emotions.

Today, we can orbit the earth's surface, yet, we cannot control our behavior patterns adequately. One of the hardest things to do is to know the 'self' and to *change* the 'self'. Even though our current knowledge of the mind is limited, it is sufficient knowledge to enable us to do this.

The 'mind' stands as an ever present challenge to 'all of us' to attempt to understand our being and in so doing, reveal the mysteries of 'self'. If we fully explore the powers of the mind and diligently apply known cosmic laws pertaining to our existence, we can soar to greater heights

29

of personal accomplishment, prosperity and happiness. Control of behaviour, mood and learning is no dream of the future. It is here now, if we so desire to meet the challenge and take charge of a creative master-piece that resides within.

Many people live under a psychic umbrella of negative information which suggests, 'destiny is in the hands of the unknown' or 'whatever will be, will be'. This attitude or concept of life is false. If it were true, there would have been little technical or social advance.

The greatest truth you can know about success is that you can control your destiny by governing your thoughts. When you take charge of your thoughts you become master of your existence.

**THE KEY TO LIFE IS WITHIN THE MIND.** The power of the human mind is almost beyond belief. Dr Norman Vincent Peale, author of the best seller **The Power of Positive Thinking** and Pastor of Marble Collegiate Church in New York City, is often quoted as saying: 'There is enough atomic energy within man's mind to blow up the city of New York.' The enormity of this hidden mind power staggers the imagination, for if this 'force' were to be fully harnessed and used by *all* men, think of the wonderful technical and social progress that could be made.

It has been estimated that man uses less than 10 per cent of his mind's potential. Albert Einstein, a recognized genius in his field, used less than 15 per cent. There is a wealth of power within, yet, man wastes 90 per cent of this power. When man learns to apply even a fraction of his true creative ability, he cannot help but succeed, for the 'real' things of life are put within his grasp: peace, harmony, happiness, health, security and prosperity. These pleasures of life are not to be found 'without' but 'within', for they stem from the *deep self* of man. *Life's riches are within the mind.* The great powers of mind are within everyone. There is a gold mine 'within' from which every man can draw all that is necessary for abundant living.

**SUCCESS IS A STATE OF MIND.** You have a first-class mind geared to efficiency but your mind will not operate successfully unless it is used correctly. If you clutter and jam your mind with false impres-sions and beliefs it will react in exactly the same manner as a computer fed with wrong information. Your mind operates in the same manner as a finely constructed machine. This is not to say your mind *is* a machine, it just works like one. The more you know about your mind the better will be your sense of direction. The less you understand, the less will be your progress and success.

Life is a 'state of mind'. You communicate through your mind to discover the world around you. And your world around you responds according to the manner in which you think, feel and believ  When you cease playing the role of 'slave' to your mind and holding to negative thoughts, ideas and feelings, you will have learned the secret of successful living.

Success is a definite state of mind—*affirmative state of mind*. Failure is also a specific state of mind—*negative state of mind*. It is appropriate to label failure 'disease' of the mind, for it manifests poor health, insecurity, poverty and a dozen or so other undesirable conditions.

**SUCCESS OR FAILURE—IT'S YOUR CHOICE.** You are blessed with freedom of choice. To choose the type of life you will lead is your God-given right.

If this were not so, you would not be capable of expressing individual talents and personality. You are free to choose an affirmative state of mind which, according to Universal Principle, will manifest the 'pleasures' of life or you may choose a negative state of mind, which manifests adversity.

The truth of your being is that God is seeking to express creativity through you, and He does this through your mind when you let Him. Your mind is an instrument of Divine Intelligence and you should be cognizant of the fact that you are able to do *all things* through the infinite and creative wisdom of your mind.

When you take charge of your thoughts, feelings and beliefs and project them in an affirmative manner, you automatically mould the success pattern of your future. *Success is a state of mind.* You control the degree of your success by controlling your thoughts.

You have the right to choose the *way* in which you will think, feel and believe. Along with this choice goes the liability of 'experiencing' what you have chosen. It's good insurance to choose to think affirmatively.

**HOW THE MIND WORKS.** The principle of any science is invisible and it is theoretical. Our idea of Spirit is theoretical. No one has seen the mind. The mind is invisible, yet it is there. No one has seen God. God is invisible, yet God is there. *God is.* No one has seen Life. *Life is* and we experience it. No one has seen Intelligence. *Intelligence is* and we use it. The mind—Spirit, Causation, Infinite Intelligence— whichever term you wish to apply to it, is beyond, yet, it is within our reach and we use it to *think* and *feel* and to *express* creative individualism.

Nature must work through man in order to work for him. It does this through man's mind. The brain is the instrument of the mind. It is made up of atoms and molecules as is the rest of the body. The brain does not 'think'. The mind 'thinks' using the brain as its instrument. The mind, being greater than the brain, rules the body. The body is the servant of the mind. Without the mind the body would cease to function.

The mind and the body are closely related. They work as one continuous mechanism. Mental energy and physical energy are also related, one assists the other. For example, proper rest of the body sharpens the intelligence or thinking powers. The mind, in turn, when operating at top efficiency, produces physical as well as emotional well being.

**THE LAW OF MIND IS BELIEF.** The law of mind is the law of belief. Belief is a thought or an idea held in the mind and acknowledged as true. The mind never produces external conditions according to facts, but according to the belief held about those facts.

This clearly indicates that man's life is governed by 'belief' or the calibre and conviction of his thoughts and ideas.

Your future is in your mind at this very moment based on your pattern of thinking. 'Think' the very best and the very best will eventuate. The mind must *actualize* what it believes to be true. That's why you should always believe that you will succeed in every undertaking. Believe it, accept it and it will happen.

**YOUR MIND IS A GIANT BROADCASTING STATION.** Your mind is like a giant broadcasting and receiving station. It is the sender and receiver of electrical vibrations or thought waves. Try this experiment. Concentrate on another person seated in the same room with you. Hold your attention on this person and silently repeat: 'look in my direction'. Your subject will become restless and respond to your wish. This is a simple yet affirmative demonstration that 'thought is energy' and can be transmitted, received and comprehended between mind and mind.

It is anticipated that within the not so distant future, a hundred years or so, man will cease to communicate via the spoken word and progress to a silent method of thought transference. In fact, successful experiments are at present being conducted in this medium. This news might throw the telephone company into panic, for mind waves know no limitations of time or space, nor are thought vibrations affected by physical barriers or distance.

**COCONUT WIRELESS MIND POWER.** The Tahitians have been using telepathy as a means of communication for many years. It is called the 'coconut wireless' and originates in the village of Papeete. When news events occur the messages are sent telepathically to natives living at other points around the island.

Dr Joseph B. Rhine, head of the Parapsychology Department at Duke University in the U.S.A., has been conducting extensive experiments which prove conclusively that extra sensory perception (ESP), telepathy, clairvoyance and telekinesis are fact. Dr Rhine has done much to make these previously 'doubtful' human abilities an accepted form of modern-day psychology.

Dr Rhine's files show ample evidence of successful mediums transmitting and receiving thoughts over great distances. Perceptive individuals are able to 'visualize' in the mind's eye past, present and occasionally future events. The ability to 'see into the future' and to receive accurate mental impressions of what is going to take place comes by way of the *superconscious* mind.

The assassination of the late John F. Kennedy was predicted by a well-known American clairvoyant. She accurately named the time, place and date the infamous killing was to occur. Unfortunately, her warning went unheeded.

**AUSTRALIAN CLAIRVOYANT PREDICTED WORLD WAR I.** In February of 1914, Mrs Foster Turner, a well known Australian medium, at a seance with Sir Arthur Conan Doyle, predicted the following:

'Europe will be deluged in blood. Great Britain will be drawn into war. Germany will be the antagonist and will totter Austria to ruin. Britain and her allies will emerge victorious.'[1] This prediction was made long before there was any whisper of a general war.

**MIND-OVER-MATTER EXPERIMENT.** Mind over matter is a reality. Among Dr Rhine's famous experiments at Duke University is one which shows that mind can exert an effect on an object without physical contact.[2] Deep concentration on a desired result before dice was tossed, brought forth the exact result each time the dice landed.

**PSYCHIC POWERS OF THE ABORIGINES.** The Australian Aborigines have amazing mind powers or so it would seem to the average person. In certain directions the aborigine is infinitely smarter than his white brother because he has learned to tap and use psychic energy. For instance, a member of a tribe who is many miles away from camp and becomes ill, is able to let his family know by sending thought messages.

An aboriginal actor I worked with on a pilot episode of an Australian TV series, told me that members of his tribe near Alice Springs have a highly developed 'sixth sense'. 'Many aborigines are mental telepathists,' he said. 'We know when a member of our tribe is sick, even though he might be fifty miles away. We know when a person is returning from 'walkabout' even if he's been away for six months. We know the exact direction he will arrive from. It is also possible to read another man's mind and know what he is thinking even though he may not say anything,' he told me. Certain tribes fire walk and my friend explained that the aborigine fire walker gains complete control over his body by directing it to the will of the mind.

---

[1] Reported by Max Freedom Long in his book *The Secret Science Behind Miracles*. Huna Research Publications, Vista, Calif.

[2] **The Reach of The Mind**, J. B. Rhine. Wm. Sloane Assoc., Inc., New York.

**FIRE WALKING BAFFLES THE EXPERTS.** The most baffling example of workable mind power is fire walking. This phenomena has been practised for centuries and is still being practised in various parts of the world. Fire walking involves bare feet, burning hot coals and a superior command of the mind. If there is trickery involved, man is yet to prove it.

This ancient ritual stands as proof that man has a great *power* that can be called upon to produce amazing feats. Although it is not the aim of this book to delve into areas of psychic phenomena, a few examples have been presented to illustrate the tremendous power of the mind over the body and over matter.

**WE ARE ALL MENTAL TELEPATHISTS.** Without realizing it consciously, all of us are involved in mental telepathy at various times during our lives. Between friends and loved ones who are apart there is often a silent communication of thoughts and feelings which can be 'picked up' by means of 'tuning in' to the mental vibrations of the other. Sometimes these mental impressions are vague, yet they are there and can be 'felt'.

As a further example of mental telepathy, consider the number of times, either at home or at work, you have thought of a friend or a business aquaintance when at that moment the phone has rung and that very person you were thinking about was the caller. This mental contact leads to the conclusion that we are part of and use a Universal Mind common to all men.

**WE ARE ALL PART OF ONE MIND.** The mind cannot be seen. It is invisible and it is Infinite. No man has seen the mind, therefore, no man has been able to isolate it within the body of man. All that is known about the mind is *what it does*, not what it is.

When we speak of 'mind' we speak of consciousness or thought, perception and awareness. Although there are three areas of the mind, there is only *one* mind and it is common to *all* men. It is *Universal Mind*, the origin of everything. Universal Mind is First Cause. It is God. Through Universal Mind there is energy and through this energy everything lives. Man's intelligence functions through Universal Mind at the level of his concept of it.

Universal Mind is an Infinite Power that does not need to be coerced into action. We do not create this *Power*, it is ever present, ever ready to work for us by working through us. When we select *affirmative thoughts*, this Indwelling Power responds by projecting our thoughts in an affirmative way resulting in affirmative external conditions. All thought has its birth in Universal Mind. We are all part and parcel of Universal Mind. It is a reminder that we are One with God from Whom there is no separation.

34

# THE THREE MINDS OF MAN

Encompassed within the *ONE* Mind.

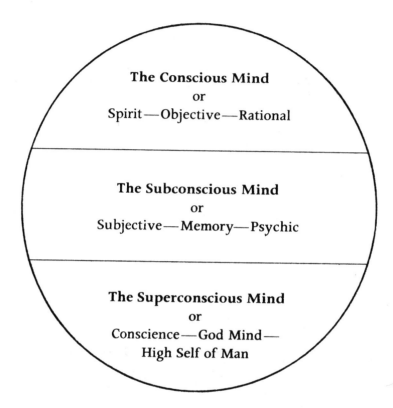

**The Conscious Mind**
or
Spirit—Objective—Rational

**The Subconscious Mind**
or
Subjective—Memory—Psychic

**The Superconscious Mind**
or
Conscience—God Mind—
High Self of Man

**THE THREE KINDS OF MIND.** There are three known levels of the mind but only *one* mind. The first level is the objective or *conscious mind* which is also called the originator. The second level is the subjective or *subconscious mind*. The third level is the High Self or *superconscious mind*.

The brain is not the 'thinker'. The mind thinks and perceives and uses the brain as its instrument. With the conscious mind man is able to *rationalize*. With the subconscious mind man is able to store all that he has rationalized and bring it back at any required time as *memory*. With the superconscious mind man is able to 'tune in' to a power greater than himself and *experience* a high degree of consciousness.

**(1) THE CONSCIOUS MIND OF MAN.** The conscious or objective mind is the *thinking* mind and the Spirit of man. Conscious mind has the ability to rationalize, but not to remember. The conscious mind cannot be hypnotized.

The conscious mind, being the reasoning mind, makes daily decisions such as the selection of clothes to wear, the type of food to be eaten, the papers and books to be read, etc. All decisions are made by the conscious mind. It gains knowledge by making use of the five senses: touch, smell, sight, hearing, taste. Whatever is rationalized and accepted in the form of 'belief' by the conscious mind is then passed to the subconscious where it is stored as information for future recall by the conscious mind. The subconscious is unable to reason whether what it has accepted is true or false. It accepts at 'face value' all that it receives. It will accept a lie as readily as the truth. This is the reason all thoughts, ideas and feelings passed to the subconscious should be of an affirmative nature. Once the subconscious accepts an idea it will bring that idea to life at some future time.

The conscious mind cannot remember a thought once it has let it go. It must rely on the subconscious to bring it back in the form of memory. The conscious mind acts as a sieve, sifting information, forming impressions, creating ideas and making decisions. Thoughts formulated in the conscious mind and passed to the subconscious for 'processing' shape destiny.


**(2) THE SUBCONSCIOUS MIND OF MAN.** The subconscious or subjective is the storehouse of thoughts, feelings and beliefs passed along by the conscious mind. It is the instrument of memory. Everything consciously thought about is stored in the vault of the subconscious. Memory is active, for thoughts can be recalled by the subconscious days, weeks or years after leaving the conscious mind.

The subconscious works with intelligence but not with self-conscious awareness. It has the ability to remember but can reason only deductively. The subconscious takes thought forms passed along by the conscious mind and forms them into future events. It actually controls and directs our entire destiny. It perceives by *intuition* and has the capacity of clairvoyance. The subconscious is amenable to suggestion and can be hypnotized.

The subconscious deals with whatever is given it in an unbiased manner, but cannot tell the difference between an actual experience and one imagined. It acts upon negative beliefs in exactly the same way as affirmative beliefs. This is an important point to remember and one worth repeating: *the subconscious mind acts in exactly the same manner toward negative thoughts, feelings and beliefs as it does toward affirmative thoughts, feelings and beliefs.* However, the outcome is vastly different.

**YOU GET WHAT YOU THINK—NOT WHAT YOU DESERVE.**
Once the subconscious mind accepts an 'idea' it immediately acts upon
it to bring forth a corresponding physical result. As a servo-mechanism
it must complete whatever it commences. The subconscious is never
pressed into action by meaningless words or surface thoughts, but by
deep feelings. *We always get what we think and believe, not what we
deserve.* Think good and good follows. Think evil and evil follows.
This is a basic law of mind and as such, is infallible. Whatever is claimed
mentally, good or evil, the subconscious accepts and brings forth at
some future time.

The subconscious, being *unimpressed* by words, but *impressed* by
genuine feelings and beliefs, will not act on surface thoughts of wealth,
health, companionship, love or happiness. There must be strong
conviction supporting desires to motivate the subconscious to go to
work on them. This is the major reason many people fail to make
affirmative thought principles work. They pound the conscious mind
with demands, attempting to force results by will power. When results
do not come, negative feelings of fear, anxiety and self doubt arise and
eventually failure is the outcome.

The most receptive time for planting affirmative ideas into the subconscious is when in a completely relaxed state and ready to go off to
sleep. This drowsy state lasts for approximately five minutes and
should be used each night for implanting affirmative thoughts of
health, happiness and prosperity into the deeper mind.

**THE GREAT TEACHERS TAUGHT THE SAME PRINCIPLES.**
The subconscious is the seat of our emotions. It also regulates the
natural functions of the body: heartbeat, breathing, digestion and
circulation.

There is a superiority of *mind over body*. We are Spirit which
motivates the body. The subconscious will never produce discord or
sickness within the body when it is in *affirmative accord* with the
conscious mind. Jesus, Moses, Isiah, Buddha, Krishna all taught this
truth. When the conscious mind is out of harmony with the subconscious—a negative state of mind—there is disharmony within the
body. Anxiety, fear and worry cause the heart, lungs and stomach to
react 'negatively'. When there is emotional disturbance, a chemical
change takes place within the system, which makes us vulnerable to
headache, backache, poor eye sight, ulcers, cancer and other illnesses.
*Sour thoughts produce a sour system.*

**YOUR SUBCONSCIOUS RESPONDS TO FAITH.** The subconscious has an 'in-built' healing principle which responds to faith.
This principle operates in much the same way as the law of *action and
reaction.* Faith is the action and the reaction is the affirmative response
of the subconscious to that faith. *'If thou canst believe, all things are*

*possible to him that believeth.'* Mark 9:23. When we have faith, our subconscious mind is influenced by our belief and desire and brings about all that we seek.

The subconscious mind is also the Soul of man. The Soul receives impressions from the Spirit or conscious mind. The subconscious is not a reasoning mind but an executor of the will of the Spirit. It is sometimes referred to as the unconscious mind. However, it is not in any sense 'unconscious' as it is always active and never rests. The subconscious mind is the power which does not reason, but which turns into reality that which has already been reasoned. It is the power that keeps the body functioning. It is the *power within* which heals and the power within which accomplishes.

(3) **THE SUPERCONSCIOUS MIND OF MAN.** Little has been written about the superconscious mind. This ever-present Spirit is man's direct link to his Creator, for the superconscious is the *God Mind* within and without. The superconscious is duality: male and female. It is the *High Self* of man.

Sri Ramakrishna, Hindu spiritual leader, used to say that when Jesus was crucified He withdrew His mind from His body. This brought him into a state of 'superconsciousness'. The nails pierced his body but not his mind. When we are 'in tune' with the superconscious nothing of an external negative nature can affect us.

The famous Swiss psychiatrist Dr Carl Jung, believed the conscience to be the spiritual part of man. Dr Jung called it the *superconscious* and maintained that it was part of a universal subconcious mind joined to God. This idea is in line with many Oriental philosophies and follows my own line of thinking.

**THE SUPERCONSCIOUS KNOWS ALL.** There is no doubt that it is possible to perceive something on a superconscious plane which is not apparent on the conscious plane. But only the superconscious can be aware of another spiritual form. Many people with psychic powers use the superconscious to 'see' into that part of the future which has become crystallized.

The superconscious uses a form of thinking greater than either reason or memory, although it is capable of both. Having a higher form of mentation, the superconscious has knowledge of the past, the present and the future.

From time to time we experience 'great moments'. We display what might be called 'creative genius' in some form or another. We are exhalted; everything seems 'right'. To experience this consciousness is to experience the power of the superconscious. This state of tranquility and creative accomplishment does not always last because we are unaware of what is really taking place within the mind. There is principle operating, but we do not know *how* this principle performs, thus leaving us at a loss to make it work on a regular basis.

The third self of man can be called upon to bring forth tranquillity, joy, happiness, peace, love and creative accomplishment. With practice, one can enter into a superconscious state by means of *meditation*. (This technique is discussed in Chapter 14). The superconscious, being part and parcel of the One Universal Mind, is ever present, beckoning us to enter into a state of 'heaven' on earth.

# SUMMARY OF IDEAS ON THE
# POWER OF THE MIND

1. *The most complex mechanism known is the MIND. It is a creative masterpiece capable of amazing accomplishment when used correctly. The more you learn about how your mind works the greater will be your accomplishment.*

2. *When you take charge of your mind in an affirmative way you are able to guide your life effectively and much more successfully.*

3. *Your mind is like a computer. If you feed it false impressions and beliefs it will react in a negative way. When you feed it affirmative ideas it brings forth affirmative results.*

4. *Success is a state of mind—***affirmative** *state of mind. There is enough power or atomic energy within your mind to blow up the city of New York. Your mind is waiting to be used efficiently and effectively.*

5. *There are three areas of the one mind:* **conscious** *or 'thinking' mind;* **subconscious** *or memory;* **superconscious** *or direct link to Infinite Intelligence.*

6. *The mind is like a giant broadcasting and receiving station. It is the sender and receiver of electrical vibrations or thought waves. It is therefore possible to read the thoughts of others and to send thought messages to others.*

# HOW TO APPLY *THOUGHT PATTERN CONTROL* TO ACHIEVE A SUCCESS CONSCIOUSNESS

## Success Ideas in this Chapter

- The PATTERN Of Thought Controls Life
- What Are Thought Patterns?
- Passport To A Rewarding Life
- An Affirmation For Success
- Cleanse The Mind Of Impure Thoughts
- Affirmative Thoughts = An Affirmative Thought Pattern
- Negative Thoughts = A Negative Thought Pattern
- Inner Thoughts Produce Corresponding External Conditions
- The Reversal Technique To Quell Negative Forces
- The Effects Of Consciousness
- The Two States Of Consciousness
- An Affirmative Consciousness Pattern Brings A Successful Life
- Think Right To Live Right
- ACCENTUATE THE POSITIVE
- Effects Of A Negative Or FAILURE CONSCIOUSNESS Pattern
- Rewards Of An Affirmative Or SUCCESS CONSCIOUSNESS Pattern
- The Effects Of Group Consciousness
- Your Best Friend Could Be Your Worst Enemy
- Choose Associates Who Help You Progress
- You Succeed With A Firm Operating Under Group Consciousness
- Why Company 'A' Fails
- Why Company 'B' Succeeds
- The Rich Get Richer And The Poor Get Poorer
- How To Acquire A MILLIONAIRE Mentality
- The More You Think Wealth The Wealthier You Become
- Control Your Present Life To Create The Future You Want
- Expert Advice To Reap Good Fortune
- Summary Of Ideas To Achieve A Success Consciousness

**3**

*All that a man does outwardly is but the expression and completion of his inward thought. To work effectually, he must think clearly; to act nobly, he must think nobly. Intellectual force is a principal element of the soul's life, and should be proposed by every man as the principal end of his being.*

CHANNING

---

**THE PATTERN OF THOUGHT CONTROLS LIFE.** *Listen not to the voice without, but to the voice within, for here, recessed in your own mind, lies the answer to your future.* Your success or failure in life depends upon the way you 'think' or the *pattern* of your thought. Poor health, unhappiness and poverty amount to failure, drawn to you by a negative thought pattern. The downward trend of your life alters when you substitute an affirmative thought pattern for a negative one. A healthy mind—*healthy thoughts*—brings about a healthy body and a healthy environment.

You are living in an intelligent universe which reacts to your state of mind. When you control your state of mind you automatically control your environment. Such is the power back of *affirmative thought control.*

**WHAT ARE THOUGHT PATTERNS?** When collective thoughts are of one group—all affirmative or all negative—they constitute a definite 'pattern' and this pattern moulds the future events of your life. It is not possible for your mind to hold two thoughts at the one time. For instance, you cannot think affirmatively and negatively simultaneously. One type of thought must hold your attention. When you let this thought go, another can then take its place. It *is* possible to think affirmatively one moment and negatively the next. People who do this are confused thinkers, poor decision makers and nervous types.

43

Affirmative thought pattern control is the answer to 'confused' thinking. It guides you to affirmative thoughts which, through repetition, form a definite pattern of thinking, which invariably leads to success in everything you undertake.

**PASSPORT TO A REWARDING LIFE.** *Thought pattern control* is your passport to a rich and rewarding life. It is a technique loaded with *power*, that can be used to increase your income, bring zestful health, peace of mind and happiness.

What's more, thought pattern control is a relatively easy principle to apply. It is *easy* because it concerns itself with *repetition* and *discipline* more than intellectual prowess. This makes it a success principle *everyone* can use with affirmative results.

To apply thought pattern control, establish in your conscious mind thoughts of an affirmative nature: peace, joy, harmony, tranquillity, love, perfection, well being, prosperity. Mentally reject all thoughts of a negative nature: jealousy, fear, anger, limitation, loneliness, sickness, frustration, poverty. When negative thoughts, ideas and feelings concerning yourself, things or other people arise, immediately reverse them and supplant affirmative attitudes.

**AN AFFIRMATION FOR SUCCESS.** Every night before retiring, repeat the following affirmation:

'My subconscious mind processes all things of an affirmative nature while I sleep and rejects all mental concepts that could be detrimental to my health, happiness and success. I will experience a greater degree of success and happiness tomorrow than I experienced today. I am a reflection of all that is *good*. I allow God to express through my mind all truths. God's peace rests and moves freely through my life. I have faith in my ability to succeed in any specific area of my work and generally in my quest for a happier life.'

These affirmations constitute a *pattern of thinking* which, if held in the mind, will manifest as external circumstance. Create a definite trend of thought—affirmative—and stick to it. This is done by disciplining the mind to accept a daily repetition of affirmative truths until they actualize in your life.

**CLEANSE THE MIND OF IMPURE THOUGHTS.** All thoughts processed by the conscious mind and held as *truth* by the subconscious —good or bad—will manifest as outer conditions at some future time. Therefore, the secret of mastering life is to cleanse the mind of all destructive attitudes, false beliefs and negative ideas and replace them with affirmative attitudes, beliefs and ideas about yourself, things and other people.

## AFFIRMATIVE THOUGHTS

=an

I will succeed in all that I set out to do.
I am punctual.
I am considerate of others.
I am honest in my dealings with others.
I am faithful to my wife (husband) and family.
I am loyal to my friends.
I am loyal to my employer.
I pride myself on my integrity.
I am truthful.
I am decisive.
I never betray a confidence.
I am enthusiastic about my work.
I never shirk responsibility.
I have the courage of my convictions.
I am confident.
I am reliable and trustworthy.
I am in excellent mental and physical health.
I applaud the success of others.
I hold genuine love for my fellow man.

## AFFIRMATIVE THOUGHT PATTERN

## NEGATIVE THOUGHTS

= a

I am hopeless.
I lack confidence.
I cannot stand to be criticised.
I procrastinate.
I am bored with life.
I am never on time.
I can't stand my employer.
I do not respect my wife (husband).
I cannot stand to be around my family.
I never seem to accomplish anything.
I try to get the best of the other fellow.
I do not care about anyone other than myself.
I do not want responsibility.
I lack ambition and drive.
I do not know where I am headed.
I drink too much.
I am overweight.
I am a gossip.
I am envious of successful people.
I hate my fellow man.

## NEGATIVE THOUGHT PATTERN

**INNER THOUGHTS PRODUCE CORRESPONDING EXTERNAL CONDITIONS.** The fundamental way to change any negative condition in your life is to change the negative pattern of your thought; you change the manner in which you think, feel and believe. There is little sense in attempting to change external conditions, you must first change *inner beliefs*, then outer conditions will change accordingly.

You are building a success or failure consciousness pattern every hour of every day. If your thoughts are negative in nature you are constructing a negative consciousness pattern and building your own bridge to failure. You reverse this condition by reversing your thoughts— substituting *affirmative* thoughts for negative ones.

*Thoughts are things;* they have tremendous power. Thoughts of doubt and fear are pathways to failure. When you conquer negative attitudes of doubt and fear you conquer failure. Thoughts crystallize into habit and habit solidifies into circumstance. You change negative circumstance by changing negative thoughts.

There is a basic law governing thought: you cannot think one thing and produce another. *Like attracts like.* Whatever the conscious mind thinks and believes, the subconscious identically creates. Jesus taught this principle 2,000 years ago, as did Buddha 500 years before that. What you *are* is a direct result of what you think, feel and believe.

Once you've made up your mind to harbour affirmative thoughts, it is necessary, by a process of repetition, to keep this pattern of thinking 'alive'. There is little to be gained by thinking affirmatively one day and negatively the next, for the subconscious works on the last thing consciously thought about.

**THE REVERSAL TECHNIQUE TO QUELL NEGATIVE FORCES.** From time to time, negative circumstance will crop up to 'test' you. Use this opportunity to put your new found 'mind power' into action. Use the *reversal technique,* reverse negative thoughts and replace them with healthy attitudes. Affirm this simple desire every time you are tested by negative circumstance: *I allow only affirmative thoughts to dominate my life. They produce all that I desire.* When you repeat this affirmation it will be taken as a command by your subconscious and obediently acted upon to return affirmative results.

**THE EFFECTS OF CONSCIOUSNESS.** Life is a state of consciousness. You *are* and you *do* in accordance with your consciousness. Consciousness is: *the state of being mentally awake to one's surroundings; the knowledge of one's own thoughts and feelings.* When you think, eat, work, play or sleep, you are expressing a part of your consciousness.

Consciousness is established at birth and develops as your learn. It is the interaction of the conscious and the subconscious. Consciousness might best be described as: *the sum total of your thoughts.* It encompasses ideas, feelings and beliefs about yourself, things and other people.

Your consciousness is an invisible computer. Attitudes and ideas fed into your *consciousness computer* manifest as external circumstances. Negative ideas and attitudes bring forth negative conditions. Affirmative ideas and attitudes bring forth affirmative conditions. Therefore, it can be said: *individual consciousness determines your destiny.*

THE TWO STATES OF CONSCIOUSNESS. There are two states of consciousness: affirmative and negative. Happiness, well being, joy and prosperity are affirmative by nature and therefore stem from an affirmative consciousness. Problems, grievances, illness, loneliness and poverty are negative by nature and stem from a negative consciousness.

Whether you acquire a negative consciousness or an affirmative consciousness is entirely up to you, for no one decrees which state of mind you must accept. Unless you have been wandering around in a mental vacuum since birth that decision will already have been made.

Your present life—negative or affirmative—is governed by your consciousness pattern. If you are unhappy, lonely, suffering from psychosomatic illnesses, a failure at whatever job you do, then you have been holding to a negative consciousness pattern and the negative conditions in your life will not alter until you make up your mind to alter the way you think, feel and believe. Your attitudes and beliefs must be of an affirmative nature if you wish to experience well being and abundance. *Be ye transformed by the renewing of your mind.* ROM. 12:2.

AN AFFIRMATIVE CONSCIOUSNESS PATTERN BRINGS A SUCCESSFUL LIFE. No man can hope to experience success while harbouring negative thoughts and beliefs. The mind has a habit of producing external conditions in accordance with beliefs. Negative thoughts and beliefs amount to a negative consciousness pattern manifesting negative external conditions. Affirmative thoughts and beliefs represent an affirmative consciousness pattern manifesting affirmative external conditions. This is the principle on which your mind works and no matter how hard you try to change it, you can't.

To maintain an affirmative consciousness pattern is to grasp the key to successful living. Take charge of your thoughts and keep them of a strong nature and new horizons will open up to you.

THINK RIGHT TO LIVE RIGHT. An attractive young widow— call her Betty James—talked to me following a lecture I gave in Sydney on 'Overcoming Problems With Humor As A Formula'. During the course of our conversation it became evident that Betty was living under a psychic umbrella of negative attitudes and beliefs. Her husband had died suddenly from a heart attack. The couple had been very much in love and the six years of happiness they shared had cemented this love to a deep degree. Now, Betty was alone and wallowing in self-pity.

She had cut herself off from family and friends and believed that 'out of respect' to her late husband she ought to live the remainder of her life in seclusion. She blamed God for his early death and told me: 'There is absolutely no reason why this wonderful man in his early forties should have been removed from my life.' This negative state of mind had taken its toll on Betty. She was bored with life, cynical, lonely, tired, depressed and suffered continually from severe headaches.

'It's better that I suffer. It's God's wish for me', she told me. I explained to her that it is God's wish that everyone be healthy, happy and prosperous and that she was no exception. We have the right to reject loneliness and bitterness and should always strive to *rise above* misfortune and heartbreak by realizing that we have the mighty power of God to call upon to see us through. Blaming God for 'set-backs' is unfair and a tragic mistake. Many times we assume that the *will of God* is something unpleasant. The will of God for every human being is to experience triumphant living.

I suggested to Betty that she change her negative thought pattern, raise her consciousness towards God and release herself from her self-imposed bondage. I also suggested that she reunite with her family and friends and as soon as possible obtain a job to keep her mind occupied. These things she did and her renewed interests in life worked wonders. Today, Betty James is once again happily married and holds a responsible position as section buyer for a large department store. Gone are former negative attitudes and beliefs which brought her pain and unhappiness. With a new consciousness pattern Betty is now experiencing a new life.

ACCENTUATE THE POSITIVE. I am partial to the song lyrics which suggest: *accentuate the positive*. Johnny Mercer wrote them many years ago and they serve as a useful reminder to do 'just that' when my own thinking is being 'tested' by negative forces.

There is little to be gained from wallowing in the slums of a negative consciousness. To do so, is to place yourself in mental bondage. You block your own progress and invite lack and limitation into your life. With the same amount of mental effort it takes to maintain a negative consciousness, you can attain a success consciousness and thereby assure for yourself health, happiness and prosperity.

The present negative conditions in your life are subject to *change* when you *change* your consciousness. It matters little whether you are the president of an unsuccessful company, the owner of a failing corner store, an unhappy housewife, a low income salesman, a life-weary pensioner, a dissatisfied student or a bored secretary; your present negative environment can be changed if you change your negative consciousness pattern. No individual or circumstance keeps you down. There are challenges and you must learn to rise above them.

If things do not seem to change fast enough, be patient. If negative thoughts, ideas and feelings creep in, reverse them immediately with affirmative thoughts, ideas and feelings. Don't worry or fret about the outcome of any given negative situation. The right result will come automatically if your consciousness pattern is affirmative; it has to, the mind always works according to principle. Determine to be optimistic at all times regardless of whatever 'forces' are trying to pull you down. Do not allow one negative thought to exist in your mind, for like a single bad speck in an apple, a single negative thought grows and spoils the 'whole'.

*Remember*: when negative thoughts, ideas and feelings crop up, recall the Johnny Mercer lyric and *accentuate the positive*.

**EFFECTS OF A NEGATIVE OR FAILURE CONSCIOUSNESS PATTERN.** A failure consciousness pattern is made up of destructive attitudes, false beliefs and negative ideas and feelings about yourself, things and other people. A failure consciousness pattern produces the following *negative* conditions in your life:

**NEGATIVE**
- unhappiness
- boredom
- loneliness
- intolerance
- lack of discipline
- poor judgement
- wrong decisions
- procrastination
- moodiness
- psychosomatic illnesses
- family discord
- marital discord
- loss of friendships
- poor business relationships
- frustration
- fear
- FAILURE

**REWARDS OF AN AFFIRMATIVE OR SUCCESS CONSCIOUS-
NESS PATTERN.** A success consciousness pattern is made up of
affirmative attitudes, strong beliefs and healthy ideas and feelings about
yourself, things and other people. A success consciousness pattern
produces the following *affirmative* conditions in your life:

**AFFIRMATIVE**
- happiness
- tranquility
- well being
- confidence
- prosperity
- youthfulness
- vitality
- enthusiasm
- peace of mind
- decisiveness
- tolerance
- patience
- marital happiness
- family unity
- improved business relationships
- wisdom
- faith
- love
- joy
- SUCCESS

**SELECT AND MAINTAIN AN AFFIRMATIVE CONSCIOUS-
NESS.** When you tally up the pros and cons of a failure consciousness pattern versus a success consciousness pattern it is obvious which
pattern is worth acquiring and keeping. Affirm every day that your
consciousness is success orientated and directing you toward your
desired goals. An affirmative consciousness *can* and *will* overcome
obstacles that may arise in your life and ensure success in all that you
do—if you maintain it.

51

**THE EFFECTS OF GROUP CONSCIOUSNESS.** Once the pattern of your individual consciousness is firmly established—negative or affirmative—you become, slowly but surely, a partner in *group consciousness*. This simply means that you attract and are attracted to other individuals who have a similar thinking pattern to your own.

It is said that: *birds of a feather flock together*. For example, a criminal type associates with other criminal types or those who think, feel and believe in a similar way. Men of high ideals do not associate with criminals because their thoughts, feelings and beliefs do not parallel.

Men of high ideals are to be found in the company of other such men. They belong to worthy business, social and service organizations. Low thinking individuals are to be found in sleezy bars and in police courts and jails . . . *and never the twain shall meet*, said Kipling.

**YOUR BEST FRIEND COULD BE YOUR WORST ENEMY.** If you stop for a moment to think about your present circle of friends you will find that their level of consciousness is on a par with your own. You will also discover that their interests and social activities correspond to yours—or else why would they be your friends? Being 'birds of a feather' you 'flock together' because of similar thoughts, ideas and feelings.

If, after analysing the consciousness calibre of your friends, you find them decisive, confident, happy and prosperous types, then you can rest assured that you are mixing with the 'right' crowd.

However, if your friends are run-of-the-mill types, lacking in personal integrity, ambition, enthusiasm and disciplined imagination, then you should take immediate steps to break away from them. This suggestion might seem a rather hard line to take, but in the long run, it will prove to be your wisest course of action, for friends who hold to a negative consciousness pattern often will—unwittingly—negate your attempts to improve your social standing and hinder opportunities to exploit your creative abilities. *You can never rise higher* than the people you associate with. Choose friends wisely and be sure they *truly* are your best friends.

**CHOOSE ASSOCIATES WHO HELP YOU PROGRESS.** You may, of your own free will, associate with whomever you wish in this world. The outcome of your 'association by choice' is always consistent with that choice. For example, if you choose to associate with 'affirmative thinkers' then your consciousness will be influenced in a progressive and right way. If it's an association with negative thinkers then their negative attitudes will slow down your progress. It takes the same amount of mental energy to 'choose friends' either way, so don't settle for anything less than the 'right' association—an association with affirmative thinkers.

52

**YOU SUCCEED WITH A FIRM OPERATING UNDER GROUP SUCCESS CONSCIOUSNESS.** When you elevate your consciousness and it is operating for you on a successful level, you naturally gravitate towards others who hold similar attitudes to your own. This often happens in the business world. For example, you might feel stymied in your present job. Somehow, the company you work for just isn't 'forward thinking' enough for you. The management lacks the drive and enthusiasm and trails the field in its particular line of endeavour. You may, because of a compulsive desire to succeed, leave this static concern and seek employment elsewhere. Your consciousness, being success oriented, pulls you toward an organization offering the potential you seek.

A success consciousness organization has a 'feel' about it. The management and employees reflect this; they are enthusiastic, forward thinking types, who seem to be a step ahead of their competitors. When you 'sense' that a company has this consciousness permeating it, join it and become part of its growth.

**WHY COMPANY "A" FAILS.** Company "A" is an automobile sales agency. On its team is a sales manager who harbours a failure consciousness—his pattern of thought is negative. Mr Sales Manager has a knack for hiring 'unsuccessful' types. These salesmen have a similar consciousness pattern to his own—*birds of a feather flock together*. No matter how hard he drives them, his team cannot match the sales record of Company "B", the competitor across the street.

The sales manager's alibis for poor sales are: 'I have poor salesmen. The opposition spends more money on advertising than we do. We are on the wrong side of the street. Money is short and people aren't spending.' What Mr Sales Manager should be admitting is: 'Our attitudes are wrong. We have to change negative attitudes about ourselves, our job and our customers.'

Attitudes or patterns of thought, constitute consciousness which directs our success or failure. Company"A" must change its group consciousness before it can expect successful group sales.

**WHY COMPANY "B" SUCCEEDS.** Let's look at Company "B", competitor to Company "A" and based across the street from its rival. Company "B" has done well since it opened for business and has an enviable sales record despite the so-called 'poor conditions' experienced by company "A".

The sales manager and sales team of Company "B" are a success consciousness group. They know they have a good product and they know there is a ready market for it. They are confident that they have the necessary selling ability to move it. What they may or may not know, is that their *affirmative group consciousness* is drawing customers of a similar consciousness pattern. These customers have money to spend. They aren't the time wasters, dreamers or wishful thinkers that Company "A" seems to attract. This affirmative group consciousness pattern of Sales Company "B" is the reason for their success.

**THE RICH GET RICHER AND THE POOR GET POORER.**
Dr Sigmund Freud, the father of modern psychology, discovered that there are basically two types of individuals: the *failure conscious* individual and the *success conscious* individual and the only difference between the two is the manner in which each 'thinks'. The failure conscious individual harbours 'defeatist' attitudes which reap corresponding results. This individual moves from failure to failure, with each 'set-back' serving to reinforce his 'belief' that he is doomed to permanent failure. The success conscious individual confidently moves ahead, building success upon success. His consistent attitude is: 'I cannot fail', and he doesn't. This theory gives credence to the adage: *the rich get richer and the poor get poorer*. The rich *think* wealth. The poor think poverty. Each gets exactly what he 'thinks'.

**HOW TO ACQUIRE A MILLIONAIRE MENTALITY.** Human behaviour experts are constantly exploring the question of why some people accumulate wealth while others do not. Dr Charles D. Flory, prominent New York psychological consultant to management, points out that wealth does not always come to the most intelligent or the most ambitious individuals, but to those individuals who 'think' money. The money thinkers have a *millionaire mentality*. They have a definite money making instinct, they are money orientated and this special attitude of mind attracts wealth to them.

Bernard Baruch, a millionaire at twenty, claims that acquiring large sums of money is a 'definite talent' like writing, music, art, etc. 'And like all talents,' says Baruch, 'it can be developed.'

In order to develop a millionaire mentality, it is necessary to look upon money, not as an end in itself, but as a desirable 'tool' to help you in the accomplishment of life-long dreams.

The money making instinct requires that you react automatically to the things that create wealth. Here is an example: Mr Brown is advised by a reliable source that a new hotel is to rise in a tourist area badly needing this service. The company supporting the venture is open to investment. Mr Brown knows that the proposed hotel cannot fail and therefore, would make an ideal investment; so invest he does.

This 'automatic reaction' to the opportunities that create wealth is the difference between Mr Brown, who sees potential and *acts* and say, another type, Mr Jones, who sees potential but lets it go because of doubts and fears. There is a big difference in *wanting* to make money and *wishing* to make money. Mr Brown 'wants' and *does*. Mr Jones 'wishes' but doesn't.

**THE MORE YOU THINK WEALTH THE WEALTHIER YOU BECOME.** It is possible to develop a millionaire mentality by thinking affirmatively about money. Be specific as to *how much* money you want and what you will do with it once you have acquired it. Have a healthy regard for money and the 'good' it can bring into your life and into the lives of others if you handle it wisely and generously. The fastest way to have wealth disappear or not show up at all, is to condemn it. Repeat every day: *I am wealthy. The riches of life are mine and I use them for the benefit of myself and others.*

Wealth is a definite mental conviction. The feeling of wealth produces wealth, for the more you 'think' wealth and affirm it, the wealthier you become.


**CONTROL YOUR PRESENT LIFE TO CREATE THE FUTURE YOU WANT.** You cannot alter your past. It has gone. Don't waste time and energy fretting over your past mistakes and missed opportunities. It is vitally important for you to understand that you can control your present and future life by controlling your ideas, thoughts, feelings and beliefs about yourself, things and other people.

Your future is your present thought grown up. Whatever you now think, feel and believe about yourself, things and other people, moulds the success or failure pattern of your tomorrow.

Your mind is Infinite Intelligence. Your duty in this life is to use this Intelligence to creatively express your talents.

The present state of your life is your own doing. Whatever enters your life is but the expression of your belief. You are not obliged to live a negative existence. No one decrees that you be sick, lonely, depressed, insecure or unsuccessful. What you think, feel and believe today, is creating your tomorrow. You build a successful tomorrow by elevating your present thoughts today. Build your future the scientific way by thinking about it, having faith in it and accepting that it is going to be triumphant.

Apply the principle of *thought pattern control* to build an affirmative consciousness; a power capable of attracting health, happiness and riches.

If you are fed up trying to cope with feelings of boredom, insecurity, inferiority; if you are plagued by ill health, failure and money problems; if you seem to be swimming upstream continually, tossed about by the raging torrents of life, then you must cease residing in the slums of your mind and immediately begin to raise the level of your consciousness.


**EXPERT ADVICE TO REAP GOOD FORTUNE.** Dr Joseph Murphy, Minister of the Church of Divine Science in Los Angeles and author of many books on the Laws of Mind, points out in **The Miracle**

of Mind Dynamics:* 'Man's joy and suffering are the reflections of his habitual thinking. The secret of good fortune is to think right, feel right, be right, do right and act right.' If you follow this sound advice you cannot help but experience joy and true happiness.

There is not one thing in your life that is or ever has been pre-determined or foreordained. Your destiny is in your own hands—or more correctly—*in your own mind*. You can create a successful future by controlling your present thoughts, feelings and beliefs about yourself, things and other human beings. You can change your life if you *really* want to. There's only *one* way that it can be done and that is by changing your thoughts and keeping them changed.

---

### The Way of the Law

All that we are is the result of what we have thought: it is founded on our thoughts . . . If a man speaks or acts with an evil thought, pain follows him . . . Hatred does not cease by hatred at any time; hatred ceases by love . . . Carpenters fashion wood; wise people fashion themselves.

from the *Dhammapada*.

---

*The Miracle of Mind Dynamics. Prentice-Hall Inc., Englewood Cliffs, N.J.

# SUMMARY OF IDEAS TO
# ACHIEVE A SUCCESS
# CONSCIOUSNESS

1. *Your mind is* **Infinite Power**. *Use this Power every day to accomplish health, happiness and prosperity.*

2. *The law of your mind is the law of belief. Believe that you can succeed and you will succeed. Have faith in everything you do.*

3. **Accentuate the positive.** *An affirmative state of mind brings success, a negative state of mind failure. You control your success or failure by governing your thoughts.* **As a man thinketh in his heart, so is he.** *THINK HEALTH. THINK HAPPINESS. THINK SUCCESS.*

4. **You** *control your destiny, not others or circumstances. Take charge of your life by using* **thought pattern control**: *every thought affirmative. To change the negative aspects of your life change your thoughts and keep them changed.*

5. *Affirmative thoughts amount to an affirmative consciousness. Negative thoughts held continually in the mind create a negative consciousness, which is to doom yourself to failure. Self management of the mind is the key to success.*

6. *You never rise higher than the people you associate with. Choose friends and business associates wisely. Select those who are enthusiastic types, those who are successful. Keep away from failures, unless you want to become one.*

# HOW TO APPLY THE PRINCIPLE OF *CHANGE* TO TRANSFORM YOUR LIFE FROM FAILURE TO SUCCESS

*Success Ideas in this Chapter*

- •CHANGE Is The Foundation Of All Progress
- •When Attitudes Change Conditions Change
- •Whatever You Sow You Will Also Reap
- •How The Gordon's Changed Their Destiny
- •Use Logic To Change Your Life
- •What Does Life Mean To Me?
- •Advertising Man Threw Off His Negative Environment
- •Three Ideas That Will Help To Change Your Life
- •Your Subconscious Mind Awaits Your Direction
- •Summary Of Ideas To Help CHANGE Your Life

*To-day is not yesterday. —We ourselves change.— How then, can our works and thoughts, if they are always to be the fittest, continue always the same.— Change, indeed, is painful, yet ever needful; and if memory have its force and worth, so also has hope.*

CARLYLE

**CHANGE IS THE FOUNDATION OF ALL PROGRESS.** I once read an article in the **Los Angeles Times** in which actor Tony Curtis said: 'I don't negate the past, but I'm not the same person I was fifteen years ago. People resent change in others because it makes them feel old. They misunderstand the need for change and development. They mistake it for arrogance and casting off one's background.'

It's true, many people do resent change, not only in their own lives but in the lives of others. They cling to the 'things of the past', rejecting new concepts and new challenges. This negative mental attitude blocks the creative processes from true expression, causing mental inertia, which is to live in a vacuum, to mentally wither and die on the vine.

Our universe is in a constant state of change. Nothing happens by chance; everything around us is subject to a perfect cycle of change according to principle: vegetation, seasons, tides, atmosphere and so on. We can foretell accurately when the sun will rise and when it will set. We know the precise time of year when leaves will fade to brown and fall. We know the exact schedule of our earth as it spins and circles the sun. We know these things because we are aware that nature operates according to specific laws.

Man, also, is governed by immutable laws. And he, as with nature, is subject to change. He must, or civilization would stagnate. *Life is growth.*

You are not the *exact* same person you were last month or last year.

61

Each minute of each hour of each day your natural function is *growth*—to expand mentally, spiritually and physically. Although you have very little control over your physical growth, you do control the rate of your mental and spiritual development, for you are free to select the manner in which to perfect your life.

**WHEN ATTITUDES CHANGE CONDITIONS CHANGE.** If you are not experiencing the life you want, it is because in the past, you have been unwilling to change negative concepts; unwilling to throw off antiquated beliefs and put into effect the cosmic laws that govern the success of your life. By failing to 'expand your consciousness', you place limitations upon your progress. Life becomes tedious. You are on a treadmill—forever circling, always returning again and again to the point of departure. This negative mental state produces insecurity, frustration, anxiety and fear, and unless changed, often leads to complete mental and physical breakdown. Once you begin to 'update' your mental ideas, you automatically begin to progress emotionally and spiritually, thus staying 'in harmony' with life and opening the way to experiencing new vistas never before dreamt possible.

**WHATEVER YOU SOW YOU WILL ALSO REAP.** The Bible teaches: *For whatsoever a man soweth, that shall he also reap.* As you sow ideas of well being, love, happiness, abundance, your subconscious goes to work on these desires and eventually brings them into your life.

Remember: *When attitudes change, conditions change.* Everything you think, feel and believe is an attitude, 'a state of mind' that constructively, can lead you to greater accomplishment or destructively, rob you of life's joys. *Thoughts are alive.* They are powerful contributors to your success or failure. When you *change* your negative thought pattern to an affirmative thought pattern, negative conditions automatically begin to change.

**HOW THE GORDON'S CHANGED THEIR DESTINY.** We were off the air. I had just completed another taping of 'Adams at Noon', a daily television program I hosted for KNXT CBS-TV in Hollywood. I headed for my office on the second floor of the administration building on Sunset Boulevard, to pick up a new script. On my desk was a stack of letters from viewers. As I leafed through them, a bulky letter of seven or eight pages caught my attention. It was from a young mother of two children living in the Los Angeles area.

'Life has lost all meaning. It has been one misfortune after another,' the letter began. 'Surely suicide would be the easiest and most justifiable end for me,' it concluded.

The young woman—we shall call Mrs Gordon—related how misfortune had driven her to the point of despair. Her husband, too ill to work, was bedridden and constantly in an irritable and unhappy frame of mind. Both the youngsters had the chicken pox and were confined to bed. With the rent overdue by three months, the landlord had served an eviction notice on the family. In addition to these set-backs, both the telephone and electricity companies had disconnected their services. Now, with barely enough money to purchase a loaf of bread, Mrs Gordon was ready to add her name to the 25 thousand other Americans, who, each year, decide 'life isn't worth it', and commit suicide.

I wrote a lengthy reply of encouragement to Mrs Gordon, stressing a complete 'change of attitude'. After mailing the letter, I telephoned a relief organization in Los Angeles and they agreed to immediately contact the family and offer assistance.

About a month later, I had a phone call from Mrs Gordon. Her attitude was one of 'joyful anticipation' of the future. 'A miracle has occurred,' she told me. 'I'm back in this business of living and can personally attest to the fact that happiness and prosperity are not myths. They can be real if you work hard at getting them,' she said.

Mrs Gordon related the entire story leading to her self-renewal. The aid society had given personal counselling to both her and Mr Gordon, offered generous financial assistance and had secured jobs for them both. The children were well and had returned to school.

Mrs Gordon went on to tell me that a miraculous transformation had occurred. 'The money was necessary, of course, it took care of our immediate problems. But more important, our whole outlook changed when we discovered that there was nothing wrong with life, just our distorted view of it. As if by magic, my husband's illness disappeared after we decided to try your advice regarding a change of attitude,' she said excitedly. 'Every night before retiring and again in the morning before rising, we held mental images of how we wanted our lives to be. We desired health, happiness and security, so we pictured these desires and we prayed for them. Almost immediately things began to change and Life took on a new meaning for us. Now, for the first time in years, we are truly experiencing a happy life.'

The Gordon's created their own 'miracle', not by chance, luck or any other superstitious nonsense, but by applying an age-old cosmic law: *cause and effect*. This law clearly demonstrates that there is no such thing as 'luck'. Everything in this universe works according to principle. For every cause there is a corresponding effect. By projecting thoughts of abundance, perfect health and happiness—*the cause*—the Gordon's experienced corresponding results—*the effect*. They changed their negative environment by changing their negative ideas.

USE LOGIC TO CHANGE YOUR LIFE. To perfect your life it is necessary to 'question', to apply logic. Question your own motives. Ask yourself: *Why am I here? Where am I going? What needs to be changed to accomplish the life I desire?* Your answers require close scrutiny.

From them, you are able to create a clear mental picture of life as it *has* been for you, what it is *now* and what it *could* be in the future. Armed with this information, you are ready to *change* those elements that have impeded your progress. With this mental blockage cleared away, you are totally free to experience a constructive, creative and happy life; the life God wants you to have.

Sit quietly and examine the three questions on: *'What does Life mean to me?'* Before writing any answers, give yourself time to 'think' about your life and what it means to you.

### ADVERTISING MAN THREW OFF HIS NEGATIVE ENVIRON-MENT.

When I first met Bob Heayes, an advertising art director in Toronto, I couldn't believe my eyes. His face was drawn and ash grey in colour. He stooped, his every moment seemed to be an effort. I guessed his age to be around fifty five. He was thirty eight. The longer we talked the more evident it became that Bob's negative thought pattern was responsible for his poor physical appearance and mental apathy.

'I'm bored with life,' he told me. 'I hate my job. It's pressure, pressure, pressure, crazy people constantly pushing me to complete this project or that project. I'd like to chuck it all and head for a quiet island and retire.'

'Retire at thirty eight? Your best years are ahead,' I told him. 'Why don't you find another job, one that would offer greater challenges, more interest?' I inquired.

'My best years are gone. I haven't the energy to start again,' he said dejectedly. I questioned him about his interests and learned that he was an avid art collector. 'I love art, not the sort of thing I'm doing for a living, but real art, paintings by the masters.'

Catching a spark of interest, I pressed the point, suggesting that he give serious thought to opening his own gallery. The idea intrigued him. He was silent for several minutes, then suddenly he jumped up, pumped my hand and said excitedly: 'It makes sense! I'm going to do it! I'm going to open my own art gallery and I'm going to make a success of it.'

About a year later, I ran into Bob Heayes in the lobby of the Waldorf Astoria Hotel in New York. He was on an art buying trip. When he stopped me I didn't recognize him. Here was a youthful looking man with a sparkling personality. 'Can't tell you how happy I've been since I opened my own Art Gallery,' he beamed. 'I'm a new man, thanks to a bright idea and a change of attitude.'

Bob Heayes accepted the challenge of a new way of life. He changed negative thoughts and ideas and supplanted them with constructive attitudes of optimism, courage and self-acceptance. He applied *logic*. Today Bob Heayes is enjoying the rewards—a successful business and a happy existence.

**THREE IDEAS THAT WILL HELP TO CHANGE YOUR LIFE.**
Negative ideas, thoughts and beliefs require affirmative change.
A correct thought pattern manifests successful living conditions. It's
as simple as that. This same principle, as used by Bob Heayes, can
change the present negative conditions in your own life if you will but
cast aside the shackles of negative thinking and apply logic: *the Science
of Reasoning.* The application of commonsense thought will work
wonders in your life. Apply it and see.

Copy the trio of *logical ideas* onto a 3 inch by 5 inch card and carry
the card with you. These *How To Succeed* ideas will help you to change
your life from failure to success.

## THREE LOGICAL IDEAS

> LOGICAL IDEA 1: *I will always have an* **open mind** *to new ideas.*
>
> LOGICAL IDEA 2: *I am willing to* **change** *my present negative ideas, thoughts and beliefs.*
>
> LOGICAL IDEA 3: *I will always adhere to an affirmative thinking principle: ideas, thoughts and beliefs of an affirmative nature.*

**YOUR SUBCONSCIOUS MIND AWAITS YOUR DIRECTION.**
Be prepared to face change with *confidence.* Don't be moulded by the
negative forces that may presently surround you. Throw off the *old*
and meet the *new* with expectation and *enthusiasm.* Tell your subconscious mind, '*I want to change and I will change my negative existence.
I want to experience all that is good.*' Repeat this affirmation several times
each day and your subconscious will take it as a direct order.

*The old things are passed away.*—11 Cor. 5:17. Move along with the
flowing, ever-changing, ebb of life. Your present life can change and be
any way you want it; but the change has to be made by *you.* What you
seek in this world begins with what you have, and what you have will
multiply when you change your negative consciousness pattern and
take hold of new beliefs, ideas and feelings about yourself, things and
other people.

It is your natural right to partake of the 'fruits of life'. These blessings
are yours for the asking: joy, happiness, health, peace of mind and
financial security. You can have them by changing your negative
consciousness pattern and keeping it affirmative.

# WHAT DOES LIFE MEAN TO ME?

*If you cannot answer all three questions, jot down whatever you can and read on. Return to this page at periodic intervals until you have answered all three questions to your satisfaction.*

WHY AM I HERE?:————————————————————

————————————————————————————

————————————————————————————

————————————————————————————

————————————————————————————

WHERE AM I GOING?:—————————————————

————————————————————————————

————————————————————————————

————————————————————————————

————————————————————————————

WHAT NEEDS TO BE CHANGED TO ACCOMPLISH THE

LIFE I DESIRE?:————————————————— - -

————————————————————————————

————————————————————————————

————————————————————————————

————————————————————————————

————————————————————————————

————————————————————————————

————————————————————————————

# SUMMARY OF IDEAS TO HELP
# CHANGE YOUR LIFE

1. **Change** *is the foundation of all progress. You progress as you change THOUGHTS-IDEAS-ATTITUDES. When you open your mind to* **new ideas** *you automatically begin to grow emotionally and spiritually. Change may sometimes be painful, yet ever needful.*

2. *When you wish to change negative conditions,* **change** *negative attitudes.* **For whatsoever a man soweth, that shall he also reap.** *Sow thoughts of love, peace, health, happiness, prosperity and you will reap corresponding results. This is the LAW OF CAUSE AND EFFECT. Think good and good follows. Do good and good is returned.*

3. *Apply* **logic** *to your life. Ask yourself the three why's: WHY AM I HERE? WHERE AM I GOING? WHAT NEEDS TO BE CHANGED TO ACCOMPLISH THE LIFE I DESIRE? Dig deep for the answers, scrutinize them, write them down.*

4. *You can't change your life until you make up your mind that you want something better. Know what you want. Be certain about it, then go after it.*

# HOW TO SUCCEED
# AT ANY AGE

*Success Ideas in this Chapter*

- •Calendar Age Is Meaningless
- •Talk Yourself Out Of Being A Failure
- •You're WASHED UP When YOU Say So
- •Accept Your Age But Change Your Circumstances
- •Best Days Are Now But Better Days Can Be Ahead
- •Look Forward To The Fruits Of Old Age
- •How To Lengthen Your Lifespan
- •The Subconscious Mind Never Grows Old
- •You Are As Young As You Think
- •Follow Cary Grant's Advice
- •Late Starters Who Succeeded—And So Can You
- •Newspaper Tycoon Began At Forty
- •Completed High School At Seventy
- •Retire From Business But Not From Life
- •What You Believe About Yourself Comes True
- •Summary Of Ideas To Help You Succeed At Any Age

# 5

*While one finds company in himself and his pursuits,*
*he cannot feel old, no matter what his years may be.*

A. B. ALCOTT

---

CALENDAR AGE IS MEANINGLESS. Medical science once had us believe that man's mental powers peaked at the age of twenty five and that at the age of sixty five he was well past his prime. The elderly were expected to retire mentally and physically and wait out their remaining days pottering around the garden or rocking away the hours on the front porch.

Today, we have more sense than to place an age restriction on man's productiveness and usefulness. Man is past his prime when he instills a negative attitude to age as 'fact' in his subconscious mind. If any man is convinced that at a certain age he belongs in a rocking chair in a convalescent home, then that is where he will end up. There is truth in the often-quoted statement: *Man thinks himself into old age.*

Calendar age is meaningless. I know youthful looking men and women in their mid eighties who act as though life is just beginning for them. These **happy** people continually express the desire to meet new friends, take on new challenges and absorb further knowledge. Any suggestion that they retire from life would be rejected. Their aim is to experience life more abundantly and this they do, helped by their refusal to 'give in' to so-called 'old age'.

TALK YOURSELF OUT OF BEING A FAILURE. If you find your-self muttering: 'I could get that job if I were the right age . . .' or 'I'll find happiness when I retire . . .' or 'I have great ideas but no sense bothering with them, I'm too old,' then you are talking yourself into becoming a failure. You are limiting your 'chance in life' because of an erroneous idea that 'age' is a deterrent to success. The only *real* chance you ever have is the chance you give yourself. You make your own breaks. Give yourself a *real* chance in life by accepting that you can experience health, happiness and prosperity at any age *if* you *believe* you can.

**YOU'RE WASHED UP WHEN YOU SAY SO.** The reason some individuals are happy, healthy and prosperous and others are not, is because the two types 'think' differently. You are 'washed up' when you believe this to be true.

Success is not limited to any one age group—not the very young, the middle-aged or the elderly; success is an opportunity presented to *all mankind*, regardless of age. Implant this truth in your deeper mind and remind yourself of it often.

**ACCEPT YOUR AGE BUT CHANGE YOUR CIRCUMSTANCES.** Those who trundle along life's highway blaming age, environment or circumstance for their failure to get ahead, are 'alibi merchants', attempting to cover up their insecurity, indifference, laziness and lack of initiative. I've yet to meet a lazy man who is a success or a successful man who is an alibi merchant.

Success is earned; so too, is failure. It takes the same degree of mental effort to reach either state. You cannot change your age, but you can create your own circumstance and environment by the way you think, feel and act. You can succeed *early* in life or *late* in life, all that is required is the *desire* to succeed and the *belief* that you *will* succeed regardless of present age, environment or circumstance.

**BEST DAYS ARE NOW BUT BETTER DAYS CAN BE AHEAD.** From the moment you accept an outdated concept of when to bow gracefully out of active participation in life, you subconsciously ease off physical and mental productiveness. You decrease your need for 'more life', instead of setting your sights on getting the most from your remaining years.

Your best days to move forward—to joyfully experience life—are *now*, but *better days*—to further enhance health, happiness and success —*are ahead*. Aim to 'get with' life, not retire from it. Remember: *Calendar age is meaningless*—unless you decree otherwise.

**LOOK FORWARD TO THE FRUITS OF OLD AGE.** The fruits of what we call 'old-age' are many: wisdom, faith, tolerance, tenderness, peace and strength of purpose. These mature happiness states are gathered over the years and are *life's reward* to us for having put in a full, true and creative existence.

What some people call 'old-age', should not be feared, but looked forward to as a time to rise to new challenges and experience new vistas of life. *Age is not the flight of years; it is the dawn of wisdom in the mind of man.*

**HOW TO LENGTHEN YOUR LIFESPAN.** Since man appeared on earth he has been the object of a biological process over which he has had absolutely no control—the ageing process. Many scientists now believe that the ageing process—partly anyway—can be controlled.

Science is attempting to find the elixir of life and perhaps one day it will. However, for now, it should be the goal of every individual to enhance the quality of his or her life by reducing the unpleasantness due to uncontrolled biological processes.

You can prevent the unpleasantness of physical deterioration by changing your mental outlook. As an example, characteristic of ageing is loss of weight. Therefore, your physical lifespan can be influenced by proper diet and exercise. You commence life with more brain cells than you use. To keep your mind alert, use your brain more. Don't be a lazy thinker. Keep your mind active. The more you use your brain throughout your early and middle years the better it will serve you late in life.

**THE SUBCONSCIOUS MIND NEVER GROWS OLD.** Your subconscious mind knows nothing of time or space, as it is one with the mind of God, which is Infinite.

Old-age is a relative term. In terms of health, sick people are old and healthy people are young. There are old young people and young old people. Your real age is determined by the way you think, feel and act. *Age is a state of mind.* You begin to deteriorate mentally and physically when you lose interest in the things that are important in life: meeting new friends, visiting new places and accepting new challenges. If you contemplate retiring from business don't let your mind and body deteriorate—stay active mentally and physically. Give attention to new ideas. Set your sights on new accomplishments. Take an active interest in things beyond yourself and your mind and body will reflect this in health, happiness and youthfulness.

**YOU ARE AS YOUNG AS YOU THINK.** Many people are under the impression that the ageing process commences around the early fifties and thereafter the mind and body deteriorate until finally senility takes over. This, of course, is not the case—far from it. Gerontologists (those who study the ageing process), point out that ageing carries out its independent process throughout the life of an individual, not just during the late years. Efficiency of nerve fibres that connect with muscles is just as good at seventy as at thirty. Therefore, we should not look upon our senior years with apprehension and fear.

*Age is in the mind;* the body reacts accordingly. To think young and to act young is to *be* young. Loss of energy, aching joints, mental deterioration can be avoided in your late years by learning early in life: *as a man thinketh in his heart so is he.*

**FOLLOW CARY GRANT'S ADVICE.** When I first met Cary Grant, I was astounded at the youthfulness of this film idol. In terms of calendar age he is well past sixty, yet, he presents a picture of a man in his forties. Grant keeps in excellent physical condition not only by regular exercise but by 'thinking' young.

Asked by a magazine editor how he managed to stay so healthy and trim year after year, Grant replied, 'I think thin'.

Follow Cary Grant's 'think' suggestion to bring order, harmony, health and balance into your own life.

**THINK** ENERGY

**THINK** HEALTH

**THINK** PROSPERITY

**THINK** LIFE ON A GRAND SCALE

**THINK** YOUNG

**LATE STARTERS WHO SUCCEEDED — AND SO CAN YOU.** You have something worthwhile to contribute to this life regardless of past failure or present age.

Almost half of the top executives in any country are between the ages of fifty five and ninety. The top echelon of government, education, religion and science is beyond middle age. Many geniuses were well past thirty before getting started. Albert Einstein, for example, was in his thirties before his mathematical genius was recognised. Grandma Moses was a late contributor to the art world; she began painting at the age of eighty. At the same age, Socrates, the Greek philosopher, learned to play various musical instruments. Michelangelo was painting masterpieces at eighty. Thomas Edison was still conducting experiments at the age of eighty. George Bernard Shaw wrote plays at the age of ninety. Robert Frost continued to write poetry until his death in 1963 — he was eighty nine. Henry Ford maintained: 'You take all the experience and judgement of men over fifty out of the world and there wouldn't be enough left to run it.'

**NEWSPAPER TYCOON BEGAN AT FORTY.** British press tycoon Lord Thompson began amassing his giant newspaper chain at forty years of age. Roy Thompson was then operating an automobile sales agency in a tiny Canadian town. Probably the biggest publisher in history—and certainly the richest—his vast enterprises include ownership of dozens of top papers in eight countries and many magazines and television stations. Now, in his late seventies, he is still acquiring newspapers and actively pushing his business interests.

Lord Thompson made more progress and money between the ages of sixty five and seventy than he made during his previous sixty five years. He can't understand a man quitting at sixty five. 'Why let good years go to waste?' is his feeling.


**COMPLETED HIGH SCHOOL AT SEVENTY.** In 1962, a 70-year-old former Los Angeles businessman came out of retirement to accomplish his lifelong goal of completing high school and college.

He attended Los Angeles Adult High School for three years, received his diploma and then went on to major in history at Los Angeles City College. Age was no deterrent to the accomplishment of this dream.


**RETIRE FROM BUSINESS BUT NOT FROM LIFE.** Those who seem to escape the general pitfalls of old-age are those who continue to work, produce and look forward to new challenges regardless of their calendar years. The quickest way to 'age' is to become bored with life. When you activate a genuine interest in your work and your surroundings, you have no time to become bored. Be an *enthusiast* for life. If you are retiring from business, don't retire from life.

The average life expectancy is three years after retirement at sixty five. This is because many retired people have no interests; they are bored with life. If you become a *participant* in life instead of a spectator, you'll find yourself enjoying life more and you'll be adding to your years.

The way you *think* and *feel*, your genuine *interest* in your surroundings, your friends, your job, are the things that keep you young in mind and body. Get an active interest in something—*anything*—and keep your life active.

Find an interesting hobby, a part time job. Join a charity organisation, a church group or club. Take an active interest to occupy your time.

Don't let your mind gather cobwebs and *die on the vine*. Remember: You begin life with far more brain cells than you use—there is always a reserve. *Use* that reserve to 'think' your way to greater health and greater happiness by becoming interested and active in some project. It will put more life into your years and more years into your life.

75

**WHAT YOU BELIEVE ABOUT YOURSELF COMES TRUE.**
Dr Maxwell Maltz in his excellent book **Psycho-Cybernetics*** explains
that when we curtail mental and social activities we become, 'set in our
ways, bored and give up our great expectations'. And, comments Dr
Maltz:

> 'I have no doubt but that you could take a healthy man of thirty
> and within five years make an "old man" of him if you could
> somehow convince him that he was "old", that all physical activity
> was futile. If you could induce him to sit in a rocking chair all day,
> give up all his dreams for the future, give up all interest in new
> ideas and regard himself as "washed up", "worthless", un-
> important and non-productive, I am sure that you could experi-
> mentally create an old man.'

Whatever you 'believe' about yourself, that belief will manifest in
one physical form or another at some future time in your life. You
begin to really experience 'life' when you allow your mind to think in
terms of 'more living' and not 'more retiring'. Think in terms of youth
and vitality, in terms of beauty and harmony, joy and happiness and
riches and prosperity. When you instill these affirmative attitudes into
your subconscious mind, your circumstance and environment respond
accordingly.

Step up to success today. Start now to *really live*. You are as young
and as successful as you *think* and *believe* yourself to be.

---

*Prentice Hall Inc., New Jersey.

# SUMMARY OF IDEAS TO HELP
# YOU SUCCEED AT ANY AGE

1. *Age is not a deterrent to success. Success is for everyone. Blaming age for failure shows you are insecure, lazy, indifferent and lacking in initiative. When you desire health, happiness and prosperity and actively go after these states—regardless of age—you will attain them.*

2. *Man 'thinks' himself into old age. You can be old at thirty and 'washed up', if you think that way. You can be successful at ninety and eager for new challenges if you 'think' and desire new horizons to conquer.*

3. *You are as old as you 'think' you are. Gerontologists point out that the ageing process carries right through your life span, not just during latter years.*

4. *The top echelon of government, education, religion and science is beyond middle-age. Almost half of any country's top executives are past middle-age. The giants of history were not teenagers but middle-aged and elderly when they hit the top. Don't retire from life because of calendar age. Your best years are* **now**, *but better years can be ahead.*

5. *The riches of life are to be found within; joy, peace, happiness, stem from your thoughts and beliefs. Youthfulness, happiness, are a state of mind. 'Think' young. 'Think' health. 'Think' prosperity.*

# HOW TO APPLY
# THE COSMIC LAWS
# THAT GOVERN LIFE

*Success Ideas in this Chapter*

• How To Experience A Life Of Positive Good
• Law 1: ENERGY
• Law 2: ATTRACTION
• Law 3: OPPOSITES
• Law 4: VIBRATION
• Law 5: GENDER
• Law 6: RHYTHM
• Law 7: CAUSE AND EFFECT
• Law 8: RELATIVITY
• Law 9: GRAVITATION
• Law 10: MIND
• Why Cosmic Laws Are So Important To You
• Summary Of Cosmic Laws

*The laws of nature are not, as some modern naturalists seem to suppose, iron chains, by which the living God, so to say, is bound hand and foot, but elastic cords rather, which he can lengthen or shorten at his sovereign will.*

PHILIP SCHAFF

**HOW TO EXPERIENCE A LIFE OF POSITIVE GOOD.** The truths regarding the laws of life are not the revelation of any one individual. The laws of life belong to the *Wisdom of the Ages*. They have been revealed to man through the years as the underlying principles from which all philosophies, religions and methods of living spring. They stem from the Infinite Mind of God. They are His laws presented to man so that he might live an orderly existence.

When man works in harmony with the laws of life he guarantees for himself health, happiness and abundance. To oppose them is to have conflict and disorder reign. Here then, is the foremost rule:

## Harmonize with the laws of life and you will experience a life of positive good.

**LAW 1: ENERGY.** *The force behind all life is energy*. The truth of this law explains that everything in the material universe is a manifestation of energy. Everything we touch, taste, smell, see, hear and think is energy. We cannot create or destroy energy but we can *change* it. As an example: we can change water into gas by means of heat.

The use of energy is centred around our thoughts which motivate activity. We 'think' and create ideas, make decisions, then churn thoughts into action. The force behind this is energy. We cannot create

81

this life force but we can change its pattern when reserves of energy are at a low ebb.

If you feel depressed, lacking in energy and require extra strength to get through a task, release the pressure valve holding your energy in store and allow this great life force to rejuvenate your system in much the same way steam escapes from a boiler. Energy is there, you are never without it. It might be sluggish at times, when your state of mind is negative or it could be vigorous, when your pattern of thinking is affirmative. When you hold to an affirmative state of mind you are in high spirits and taking advantage of the life force that is within.

As an example of the power that is energy, take the amazing case of a 76-year old New Yorker, who ran amok and withstood a half-hour tear gas attack and battled ten policemen with his fists, before he was subdued. He emerged unscathed from the battle but sent four policemen to hospital. A police spokesman said it was like fighting twenty men with the strength of giants.

Another case of amazing energy (and the wrong use of it), concerns a man who ran amok in Manhattan and fought off twenty policemen before he was overpowered, handcuffed and put in leg chains. 'The man was like a steamroller,' is the description of the incident given by police.

Other energy feats have been recorded of people lifting automobiles from accident victims, of bending iron bars, of wrestling bears and alligators when life and limb were threatened. Energy is power. It is a strength we can call upon to see us through when we are mentally and physically 'down'.

Man has harnessed the materials above and below the earth's surface to give him sources of energy. He has uncovered the secrets of the storm and used his vast knowledge to reach the moon. Yet, man has over-looked the greatest power potential of all — the energy residing within his own being.

There are vast amounts of untapped energy lying dormant within everyone. Enjoy life more by calling upon your unlimited reserves of energy. Release the valve and allow the life-pressure to surge through your system rejuvenating your mind and body for health, happiness and greater accomplishment. Controlled energy multiplies your power to get from life that which you most desire. It is the driving force behind all monumental accomplishment.

LAW 2: ATTRACTION. *In seeing the end result of a goal, the means to the accomplishment of the goal is created.* This law demonstrates that man attracts to him the necessary elements for the accomplishment of goals, if he is able to *see* and *feel* the reality of his desires.

As an example of the application of this law and its success, I remember an attractive young woman who attended one of my lecture courses on television acting and commercial presentation in Hollywood. She was an extremely timid and shy girl, yet, she wished to become a fashion and photographic model—a profession that requires a high degree of self-confidence. During the first week of the training program, I felt that unless her shyness was replaced by a confident belief in her ability to succeed, the young woman wouldn't have much hope of success in the competitive world of modelling. I pointed out this fact to her and asked how much her goal really meant. 'I want it more than anything else in the world,' she told me. Knowing that she was determined to succeed, I presented her with a number of books on self-confidence and personality development. I also gave her an assignment, to speak before the class each week on why she wanted to be a model and how she intended to attain her dream. On several occasions, when called upon to rise and present her three minute assignment to the class, she got to her feet, turned a bright crimson and fled from the classroom. As the weeks went on, the young girl began to enjoy her 'confidence' exercise. Her fellow students helped by applauding generously and praising her efforts. By the end of the 26-week course, I found it difficult to get the once shy and timid girl to stop speaking. She had gained self-confidence by degrees. Each speech brought her closer to the realization that she already possessed the *ability* to confidently get up in front of an audience, all that was needed was a willingness to develop it. And this she did.

She later told me, that every night prior to sleep, she created a mental picture of herself standing before the class confidently delivering a speech. She also visualized herself as a model parading before the public in beautiful clothes.

The sequel to this story is an interesting one. After taking training at a modelling school, the young woman answered an advertisement in the Los Angeles Times placed by a clothing manufacturer seeking a house model. Nearly two hundred girls applied for the job, most of them highly experienced models. Our shy young friend got the position, because, as her employer put it, 'she talked me into it and won me over with her self-confidence and charm of manner'. Her bright personality and modelling ability so captivated this manufacturing executive that he sent the girl to New York to head his newly established fashion house. The once timid young lady, is today, a top New York model and fashion executive, earning a salary in the vicinity of $22,000 a year.

This young woman applied the law of attraction. She 'imagined' and 'felt' the reality of being a top fashion model. She sustained the idea, convinced that the means to the end would arrive and fulfill her dream.

Apply the law of *attraction* to get affirmative results in your life. Feed your subconscious with definite ideas of what you want. Visualize yourself in the role you wish to play in life. Your subconscious will respond by finding *the means to the end*, attracting more health, more prosperity and more happiness.

**LAW 3: OPPOSITES.** *Things come in pairs.* All opposites are the same in nature but differ by degree. They are dual expressions of one principle. There is a positive and negative effect on all things. For example, a fire to a hiker lost in the bush is his means of warmth and comfort—a positive force. Another fire raging uncontrollably through a community brings destruction and havoc—the negative opposite. Knowing that there is a positive and a negative side to everything gives us hope for better things to appear: sunshine following rain, a smile following tears, perfect health following sickness. Realizing that ill-health has as its opposite well being, encourages us to confidently work for a state of well being by controlling negative emotions such as, fear, anxiety, tension and worry.

The law of opposites might also be called *polarity* or the law of *substitution*, knowing that something good can be *substituted* for something of a negative nature. When we apply this law by calling for the *positive opposite* to the negative situation, we can expect: good for evil, pleasure for pain, confidence for fear and love for hate. The law is a *just* law and operates for a definite purpose or else how could we ever get to know the 'opposite' to what we now experience? It would be a strange world indeed, if we were not able to experience a state of happiness after having experienced a state of unhappiness.

Whenever negative conditions enter your life apply the law of opposites: substitute the affirmative opposite for the negative condition.


**LAW 4: VIBRATION.** *All things are in motion.* Everything vibrates. The solid table is whirling electrons charged with energy, each electron in orbit. All matter regardless of apparent solidity, is made up of atoms that, in turn, are made up of protons around which electrons are spinning.

We can use this principle to advantage by realizing that vibrations can be transmitted from one person to another in the form of thoughts and feelings. Humans radiate a magnetic energy, revealing their true personality which others can sense. Highly sensitive mediums can 'pick up' mental impressions and messages transmitted by others at a distance. It is assumed that the brain radiation responsible for the transmission of thoughts occurs on wavelengths in the centimetre, millimetre and micron ranges. Scientists eventually hope to create a brain wave amplification device for communication between humans. There is nothing supernatural about this. Everything occurs by cosmic law. Mental telepathy is within the reach of those who train the mind in this direction.

Understanding that everything is in motion and 'balanced' in the universe, gives us a clue in the care of the mind and body. When we are 'out of sorts', it is because our thought vibrations are negative. We are 'off-balance' with nature. We are projecting negative *attitudes* that return negative *circumstance*, which in turn, brings about highly destructive emotions such as: fear, frustration, anxiety, jealousy, hate and hostility. Refrain from projecting negative vibrations in the form of negative thoughts and feelings.

**LAW 5: GENDER.** *There is male and female principle behind all creation.* The masculine and feminine principle gives rise to a third form. Relating this principle to our goals, we find that 'ideas' originating in the conscious mind, (male principle) and accepted by the subconscious, (female principle) are brought to life in the form of *the action* that takes place. It is important to sow thoughts of an affirmative nature, for as they are accepted by the subconscious they are born as *affirmative conditions*. In like manner, when the subconscious is impregnated with negative thoughts, negative conditions are born into your life.

**LAW 6: RHYTHM.** *Everything in the universe is in perfect balance and rhythm;* seasons, tides and even our emotional moods, when we adhere to a constructive pattern of thought. We all experience 'down days', when we have fits of depression, moodiness, self pity. When a negative state of mind occurs we are physically and mentally off-balance and out-of-rhythm with the orderly rhythm of things around us. It is possible to get back into the rhythm of things by reversing the pattern of thought. *Accentuate the positive* and *refuse* the negative. Nature is harmonious and balanced. When negative feelings are turned aside, life remains in rhythm and balance. Harmonize with nature, balance your life with healthy thoughts, feelings and beliefs.

**LAW 7: CAUSE AND EFFECT.** *Every cause has its effect.* Other descriptive terms might be: 'sow and reap', 'give and get', 'action and reaction'. This law establishes clearly that there is no such thing as 'chance'. Everything in this life is definite. Whatever you do and say, returns to you in a like manner. This law works on the mental, physical and spiritual planes. It is a means whereby man must learn that any act of evil conducted on his part, will be returned to him in a negative way at some future time. An act of charity is always returned as such.

The law of cause and effect is one of fair play. It is just and it commands respect. Choose thoughts and actions wisely, for you will *reap what you sow*.

**LAW 8: RELATIVITY.** *All things are relative.* Everything we now know, is related to something else. We can apply this law to our lives by realizing that there is a direct relationship between the thoughts we think and the acts we perform. Examine an idea before it becomes a situation in your life. See your idea in *true perspective*—as it *really* is, not as it *appears* to be. By applying the law of relativity, not so much from Einstein's point of view which deals with matter, but from the mental plane, you are able to gain true perspective and so control outer circumstance.

85

As an example, we are told that too much fat in our diet is unhealthy and causes various stomach disorders. Try telling this to an Eskimo, whose diet is fish and blubber. I'm quite sure Eskimos would have to take stomach remedies if they were to be brainwashed into accepting the idea that 'fat is harmful'.

The form in which food is eaten makes little difference to the inner chemistry of the body. The diet of fish and blubber of the Eskimo, is healthy, because he believes it to be so. Give the same diet on a regular basis to an American, who believes excess fat will cause him to have a heart attack, and more than likely he will experience one. This may cause a few hearts to flutter in medical circles, but I would rather believe that man creates ulcers, heart attacks and various other illnesses, because of the way he 'thinks and feels' about himself and his environment, rather than what he eats. It is a matter of looking at things as they *are*, instead of how they *appear*.

LAW 9: GRAVITATION. *Gravitation is to tend towards a centre of attraction.* The law of gravitation does not allow for a solid object to remain suspended in mid-air without means of support. Objects always return to the *centre* of attraction. Use this principle to attract health, happiness and prosperity. An affirmative thought pattern produces an affirmative consciousness, which is to make your being the *centre of attraction* to which all things affirmative gravitate. Affirmative emotions attract a healthy mind and body; affirmative actions attract happiness and prosperity.

Establish a mental picture of yourself as a 'centre' to which all affirmative things gravitate. Draw an imaginary circle around yourself and allow only the 'good' things of life to enter, thus enhancing your existence. Your affirmative state of mind will attract *health*, not sickness; *confidence*, not fear; *love*, not hate; *riches*, not poverty; *joy*, not unhappiness; *success*, not failure.

LAW 10: MIND. *The law of mind is the law of belief.* The greatest treasure you can possess is a healthy mind. Everything that happens in your life begins as a thought in your conscious mind. When man comprehends the creative law of mind, he ceases to blame others and outer conditions for unhappiness and failure. He becomes aware that the calibre of his own thoughts creates his destiny. There is no power in anything. The power is within man's mind—the way in which he thinks, feels and believes.

The mind is individualized in us, therefore we can lead a unique life by projecting individualized affirmative thoughts and *believing* in them. When you activate the wisdom of your deeper mind and allow it to flow freely in your life you experience happiness and the fulfilment of your desires.

You have the power within your mind to override all obstacles. You gain the consciousness of success by applying the law of your mind which is the law of belief. As you think, feel and believe, so will be your outer circumstance. What you *are* and what you *have* are both linked to the calibre of your *thought* and *belief*. *Know* that the law of mind is one of belief. *Practise* the law of mind by disciplining your thoughts. *Express* the law of mind through the co-ordination of your actions. *In belief lies the secret of all valuable exertion.*— BULWER.

**WHY COSMIC LAWS ARE SO IMPORTANT TO YOU.** There are natural forces operating throughout the universe which react and change the nature of the physical body and react upon the mental capabilities.

The ten principles outlined in this chapter, while not exclusively laws of mathematics, physics and chemistry, are cosmic laws that have a direct bearing on your success or failure. The laws of mathematics, physics and chemistry differ little from the laws of your subconscious mind. The subconscious is principle, as is everything, and therefore, operates according to principle.

The reason so many people are in conflict with themselves, things and other people, is because they misuse the laws of life. Laws govern our existence. We cannot escape them, for there is principle working through everything we come in contact with: seasons, tides, food, machinery, the automobile, the aeroplane, the ship, etc.

The laws of the universe are not in conflict with one another. But man, more often than not, is in conflict with the laws. Head down, back bent, braced against the winds of logic and reason, he attempts to get things the easy way, by conniving or using dishonest methods. The law of cause and effect sees to it that man gets back exactly what he gives.

To attempt to do battle with cosmic laws is foolhardy. No one, yet, has been able to plant an apple seed and bring forth a banana; it is contrary to principle—*like attracts like*. Cosmic laws operate through everything, perfecting everything. Observe how the laws of life function in the arts, sciences and professions. Experience is only useful when you seek and find the *true* reason for the incident. Observe the laws, obey the laws and you will *enhance* your existence.

# SUMMARY OF COSMIC LAWS

1. **ENERGY**—*The force behind life is energy. There is always an abundance of energy at your disposal to complete every task regardless of how 'down' you may feel. You can change sluggish energy for vigorous energy, by calling upon your reserves of energy stored within your system.*

2. **ATTRACTION**—*In picturing the end result of a goal, the **means** to the end is created in your subsconscious mind. Attract the **means** to accomplish the end result by feeding the subconscious definite thoughts of what you want in life. Picture yourself in the role you wish to play and affirm in your mind that you are capable of success.*

3. **OPPOSITES**—*Everything has its pair of opposites. All opposites are the same in nature but differ by degree: sickness and health, poverty and wealth, good and evil, etc. Whatever you experience in life always has its **better** side. Therefore, you can expect to experience **sunshine** following rain, **happiness** following loneliness, etc.*

4. **VIBRATION**—*All things in this universe are in constant motion. Everything vibrates. Electrical vibrations emanating from the brain in the form of thoughts, can be picked up and read by highly sensitive mediums. Mental telepathy is within the reach of those whose minds are trained in this direction. If you are feeling 'blue', you are projecting negative vibrations. Others are able to 'sense' your negative or affirmative vibrations.*

5. **GENDER**—*Two things produce a third. Thought forms created in the conscious mind and passed to the subconscious, manifest in physical form at some future time. Good thoughts manifest good conditions, negative thoughts negative conditions.*

## Summary Of Cosmic Laws—continued

6. **RHYTHM**—*Everything is in perfect balance and rhythm in the universe. When negative conditions control your everyday affairs you are out of balance with life around you. An affirmative thought pattern keeps your emotions in balance.*

7. **CAUSE AND EFFECT**—*There is no such thing as 'chance'. Whatever you sow in life you also reap. For every cause there is always a corresponding effect.*

8. **RELATIVITY**—*There is a direct relationship between the thoughts we think and the acts we perform. Look at your thoughts, check them before they manifest as outer circumstance in your life. See situations as they really are—*in true perspective—*rather than as they* appear *to be.*

9. **GRAVITATION**—*Use this principle to attract the good things of life. Establish a mental picture of yourself as a 'centre', toward which health, happiness, riches, gravitate. Your centre of gravity will be strong if your consciousness pattern is an affirmative one.*

10. **MIND**—*If you desire peace of mind, health and prosperity, you will get it if you apply the law of mind which is* belief. *You win success by believing you* can *succeed. Your life is guided by what you believe to be true about yourself, things and other people. Belief is the power behind all great accomplishment.*

# HOW TO APPLY THE *BIG 5 INDIVIDUAL MOTIVATORS* THAT MAKE YOU A SELF POWER

## Success Ideas in this Chapter

TELEPHONE 703 435-4434

REG. NO. AB6048640

JAMES B. BLITCH, JR., M. D.

1810 MICHAEL FARADAY DRIVE

RESTON, VIRGINIA 22090

NAME Asma Majboor

AGE

ADDRESS

DATE 3/30/98

R̶

Effexor 75mg XR

Sig: 1/1 P.o. qAM

Disp: # 90

J. Blitch M.D.

SIGNATURE OF PRESCRIBER

☐ DISPENSE AS WRITTEN

☐ VOLUNTARY FORMULARY PERMITTED

"IF NEITHER BOX IS MARKED, A VOLUNTARY FORMULARY PRODUCT MUST BE DISPENSED."

# 7

*The greatest results in life are usually attained by simple means and the exercise of ordinary qualities. These may for the most part be summed in these two—commonsense and perseverance.*

FELTHAM

---

**DISCOVER THE SUCCESS TECHNIQUES OF FAMOUS PEOPLE.** During my six years as a newspaper editor-publisher in Toronto, and ten years as a TV and radio broadcaster in the United States and Canada, I had the opportunity of interviewing many successful men and women from all walks of life: religious leaders, politicians, entertainment stars, business and professional figures, educationists and scientists. I discovered that by asking these prominent individuals the 'right' questions and carefully screening their answers, I was able to learn many valuable success formulas. In analysing the lives of these people, I found that without exception all utilized 'individualized' techniques to achieve success. Without exception, these techniques or *motivators* were diligently applied to overcome problems, make important decisions and obtain specific goals.

**WHAT ARE MOTIVATORS?** *Motivators* are ideas or techniques that play a significant role in the attainment of desired goals. They are success principles that incite *action*. Motivators have definite purpose and once 'believed-in' and diligently applied, bring forth affirmative results.

The 'individual' motivators presented in this chapter have been tested and proved workable by five successful men. They are simple, yet effective mind power principles that put you in the right frame of mind to attract happiness and prosperity.

## INDIVIDUAL MOTIVATOR 1: *POSITIVE ASSUMPTION*

**A SALESMAN USED THIS TECHNIQUE TO EARN $25,000 A YEAR.** I well remember the successful selling technique of Joe, a Toronto advertising space salesman. His remarkable record of selling nine out of every ten prospects was due to the application of *positive assumption*. I spent several days making the rounds with Joe a couple of years ago, in order to learn the secret selling motivator that still nets him about $25,000 a year.

After watching Joe in action, it was evident that he never tried to 'aggressively sell' any of his prospects. He did the 'spade work', as he called it, in his conscious mind prior to approaching the customer. He went through the mental gymnastics of the sale the night before or seated in his car outside the prospect's office. Convinced that the sale was already 'in the bag', Joe then introduced himself confidently to his prospect. 'Mr Smith', he would begin, 'you've got the finest merchandise manufacturers can produce, now let's prepare an effective advertisement so that everyone in town knows about it besides you and me.' This was Joe's 'technique'. He never asked a prospect 'would he buy', he acted as though the customer had already said 'yes'. This individualized success technique Joe called: *positive assumption*.

'When you try to "sell" a client, you automatically give him an opportunity of saying "no", Joe told me. 'I make the sale in my mind first. I hear the customer saying, "good, let's go ahead", then I walk into his premises and get him to sign the contract.'

This technique—positive assumption—took Joe many months to perfect. It cannot be used in an arrogant way or without firm conviction and confidence in the technique itself. It requires an affirmative attitude to 'influence' the consciousness of the person you are dealing with. If Joe approached prospects harbouring doubts and fears his selling record would not be as effective.

Never undertake any task thinking defeat. Apply Joe's individualized motivator—positive assumption—and back it with FAITH. *As the flower is before the fruit, so is faith before good works.*—WHATELY

## INDIVIDUAL MOTIVATOR 2: *VISUALIZATION*

**HENRY FORD USED THIS TECHNIQUE TO BUILD HIS DREAM CAR.** Henry Ford used the art of *visualization* to commence what has now become the second largest automobile company in the United States. Ford 'pictured' in his mind's eye the type of automobile he wanted to build at a price most people could afford. He created a *mental* blueprint of his dream car long before it was ever put to paper. Then he pictured great numbers of people buying and driving it. The idea of a low-priced car was reasoned by his conscious mind as 'feasible'. It was then accepted by his subconscious as 'an undertaking to be accomplished'. It was only a matter of time before Ford's 'vision' became a reality. Perhaps you're driving an up-dated version of Henry Ford's 'brain child'.

**THINK UP YOUR OWN MENTAL MOVIES.** The father of American psychology, William James, pointed out that the subconscious mind will bring about any mental picture when it is supported by strong belief. James maintained that the easiest way to formulate an idea and eventually bring it to pass is to 'visualize' it in the mind's eye. Hold a mental picture of what you want, day and night and *believe* in it until it becomes a reality in your life.

I have used James' suggestion, coupled with the individualized technique of Henry Ford—visualization—for many years and with affirmative results. Prior to any important undertaking I use the time prior to sleep to 'flash' on the screen of my mind the exact outcome of my desire. If it happens to be an acting role, I visualize projecting the character I am playing to the satisfaction of the director. I see the stage play or film playing successfully in theatres.

**VISUALIZATION AND STRONG BELIEF AVERTS DISASTER.** Prior to returning to Australia in 1967 to host the Tonight Show for Sydney's Channel 10, I produced a stage play in Los Angeles with a large Hollywood cast. Many problems arose which threatened to disrupt the production. The situations involved Actors Equity, the refurbishing of the theatre which was behind schedule, and the actors themselves, many of whom were playing at being slightly 'temperamental'. Opening night was booked to capacity with Hollywood producers, casting directors, agents and reviewers. A champagne press reception had been planned to follow the performance, yet it looked as though the final construction of the theatre would not be completed in time to open. I spent every spare moment 'visualizing' each problem dissolving and the opening night being a social and creative success. I backed my mental picture with strong belief that the play would succeed in every way. True to the principle, every problem did dissolve. The reviews were highly complimentary and the entire opening was the success I had desired, pictured and believed in.

**NAPOLEON USED VISUALIZATION.** Napoleon practised soldiering in his imagination before going into battle. He knew exactly what moves he would make and anticipated in his mind's eye how his enemy would react.

Visualization is capable of playing a bigger role in your life than you might imagine. Mental pictures offer a chance to 'try out' things before you put them into practice. For instance, you might wish to use the visualization technique to gain a new job. Play through the interview in your mind. Flash it on your mental screen. Go through the anticipated questions that might be asked and rehearse the answers. See yourself being accepted, happily shaking hands with your new employer and commencing your new position.

**MASTER OF GREEK SHIPPING DREAMED OF OWNING FLEET.** Aristotle Onassis, the Greek shipping king, dreamed of owning ships as a youth. In his mind's eye, he saw himself as the owner of a large fleet of cargo ships. In 1930, his vision became a reality. Onassis bid $120,000 for six 10,000-ton Canadian National Railway ships, which was no more than one-per cent of their original cost. It was during the depression years and because of the slump, Onassis was successful in his bid.

Today, along with his sizeable investment in Olympic Airways and miscellaneous other interests, Onassis commands huge 100,000-ton supertankers that are part of his 90-ship tanker and freighter fleet. Onassis reportedly controls assets whose value is reaching the $1 billion figure.

**CONRAD HILTON VISUALIZED OWNING HOTELS.** When Conrad Hilton was in his teens, he pictured himself as an important hotel operator. Hilton 'visualized' the hotels he wanted to own.

A mental picture of a desire is another form of prayer. It is a strong wish for 'good' to take place. When you hold a picture in your mind's eye of what you want in life or what you wish to become and you back it with faith, it will come to pass. *All things, whatsoever ye shall ask in prayer, believing, ye shall receive.* MATT. 21:22.

Individualize the Henry Ford motivator—*visualization*—and use it to project your dreams. Practise flashing on your mental screen the situations you wish to overcome, the interviews you wish to be accepted on and the type of person you desire to be. Do it often—practise makes perfect.


INDIVIDUAL MOTIVATOR 3: *AFFIRMATIVE REPETITION*

**HENRY KAISER BUILT A $3-BILLION EMPIRE ON THIS TECHNIQUE.** Henry J. Kaiser, the 'miraculous shipbuilder' of World War II, started work as an office boy and eventually headed an industrial empire in the U.S.A. worth nearly three billion dollars.

During the war, Kaiser was best known for the amazing production feat of turning out a liberty ship or small aircraft carrier a day. His huge industrial empire embraced dozens of industries including steel, cement, aluminium, construction, hospitals and a radio and television station in Honolulu. Kaiser was known as the boldest industrialist since Henry Ford. He forged a success path with drive, imagination and a tremendous capacity for work.

Henry Kaiser used the art of *affirmative repetition* to implant in his subconscious mind the idea that every undertaking would have a successful outcome. To Kaiser, it was a foregone conclusion—positive assumption—that each new project would succeed, with no 'ifs', 'ands' or 'buts'. He made a regular practice of repeating to himself, 'I am a success. This new undertaking will succeed'. Kaiser's 'individualized' success technique—affirmative repetition—is another term for auto-suggestion. It matters little what it is labelled, the fact is, it works. And it will work in your life if you apply it and support it with a firm belief that it *will* work.

To affirm anything is to state that it is so, that it has a basis of truth. This does not mean to say that if you vainly repeat a specific desire it will come forth as if by magic. Vain repetition is not the answer. Your desire must be a sincere request backed by faith. There must also be an affirmative conviction that the thing 'hoped for' is *right*, is *needed* and therefore will come to pass. This is the intelligent application of the motivator *affirmative repetition*.

Repetition is a potent force in sinking a suggestion into the subconscious. *Implant* thoughts of *prosperity*, if wealth is what you are seeking. *Implant* thoughts of *perfect health*, if health is your immediate concern. *Implant* thoughts of *joy* and *love* if happiness is your immediate goal.

Make this simple affirmation and repeat it often:

> *Happiness, well being and prosperity are now entering my life. I experience radiant health. I experience peace of mind, joy, love and happiness. I experience new found riches and give thanks for them as they enter my life this very day.*

Believe that after a suitable incubation time your desires will come to pass. Never negate the good your affirmations can do by 'doubting'. As soon as you begin to wonder why results aren't coming as quickly as you imagined, you set up a reversal of the principle you are using.

THE RULE:

*Don't counter an affirmative suggestion with a doubt or you will negate what you consciously desire. Change 'fear' of the outcome into 'belief' of success.*

INDIVIDUAL MOTIVATOR 4: *BULLDOG TENACITY*

**THOMAS EDISON'S TECHNIQUE TO OVERCOME 10,000 FAILURES.** Thomas Alva Edison used the art of perseverance or *bulldog tenacity*, to succeed. This great scientist was a master strategist in overcoming failure. It has been estimated that Edison fought through ten thousand set-backs before perfecting the electric light. Whenever a problem plagued him, he would lie down and take a cat nap. Rising refreshed a short time later, he would eliminate his previous approach to the problem and try a new one. If this proved unsuccessful, Edison repeated the procedure. He worked relentlessly on overcoming the 'problem at hand', believing that each failure would bring him that much closer to success. The more failures, believed Edison, the more he learned what 'not to do' the next time.

One of Edison's greatest set-backs was the loss of his prized laboratory worth millions of dollars when the building was gutted by fire. Important notes were burned and valuable equipment destroyed. Added to this, Edison carried no insurance on the building. It was felt the shock would be too much for him when informed of the catastrophe. Not Edison, 'We'll start rebuilding tomorrow', was his courageous reply.

Edison possessed bulldog tenacity; he hung on, he persevered until he won. This great man had a simple faith and a profound love for his work, never letting from his sight his fondest dream—successful experiments to aid mankind.

**BE PATIENT BUT BE PERSISTENT—WHEN ONE DOOR CLOSES ANOTHER ALWAYS OPENS.** Difficulties are opportunities for progression to better things; they are stepping stones to greater experience. Perhaps someday you will be thankful for some temporary failure in a particular direction. When one door closes, another always opens; as a natural law it has to, to balance.

Any difficulty which confronts you today can be overcome by refusing to 'give in' to the problem. Something has told all famous people to 'keep going'. Running away from difficulties only brings equivalent obstacles at some future time. Apply the Thomas Alva Edison motivator—bulldog tenacity—to overcome difficulties as they arise. Don't run away from them, stay and fight them. Be patient, but be persistent. Don't waste time over silly egoistic regrets. Reach up, grab hold of another rung of the *ladder of life* and keep going.

*. . . as the springs return—regardless of time or man—so is HOPE! Sometimes but a tiny bud that has to push up through the hard shell of circumstance to reach the light of accomplishment. Do not give up HOPE!—* DOROTHY MILLER COLE.

**IF IT'S WORTH HAVING IT'S WORTH FIGHTING FOR.** When you have the determination to overcome obstacles you will. Too many people give up too soon. If things aren't forthcoming as quickly as anticipated, don't use it as an excuse to quit. I can't remember who said it, but it's worth repeating: *A quitter never wins and a winner never quits.* Spasmodic efforts are a waste of time. Anything worth having, is worth fighting for. When you believe in something and you want it, go after it. Give persistent attention to it and you will get it. Be determined; persist until the thing 'dreamed of' is yours. Remember: *for every need where there is persistent endeavour, there is eventual fulfillment.*

If you wish to succeed, to live the 'good life', then you must be willing to undergo hardship for the sake of your desired goals. You must have the willingness to persevere until your dreams become a reality. If you are experiencing temporary defeat at present it could be because your plan of action is unsound or your attitude toward the problem at hand is wrong. Check out the problem and reason it out; there is an answer. No man is ever whipped until he quits in his mind. Success waits just one step beyond the point at which defeat overtakes you. Persist, hang on, determine that defeat is temporary and success is awaiting your next step.

A salesman friend of mind has this motto framed and sitting on his office desk: *I will never quit because men say no. I will use that 'no' as a stepping stone for a 'yes'.*

**A FAMOUS PIANIST PERSEVERED AND FOOLED HIS DETRACTOR.** Roger Williams, the popular pianist, did not get serious about music until a teacher told him, 'You will never amount to anything but a music teacher.'

'That's when I started practising ten hours a day. I had a tremendous desire to be famous. I wanted to be the greatest pop pianist who ever lived,' said Williams.

Williams' desire and determination paid handsome dividends, for today he is not only the largest-selling pianist in recording history but also the largest-selling instrumentalist of any sort. Williams' records to date have topped the 15 million mark. Not bad for a young man who was told he would never amount to anything more than a 'music teacher'.

**FROM RAGS TO RICHES.** Negro 'soul' singer James Brown, who once shined shoes outside a radio station in Augusta, Georgia, now owns the station. Not only that, he owns a Rolls Royce and five other luxury cars, a music publishing company and various other enterprises. It's estimated Brown is worth in the vicinity of $4 million. From rags to riches, from poverty to success, is no fairy-tale in the case of James Brown. 'Poverty teaches you to use commonsense, to make a masterpiece of your life. You have to persevere if you want to succeed,' is the singer's advice.

**ONE OR TEN THOUSAND DEFEATS—KEEP GOING.** Bulldog tenacity is essential if you wish to succeed in this competitive world. Napoleon maintained, 'victory belongs to the most persevering'.

Decide right now to use every set-back as a stepping stone to a subsequent success. Defeats can be valuable to you if you learn from them. Study set-backs, find out the 'why?' in them. Use them as guideposts to help you turn defeat into success. Remember: *defeat is a state of mind.* The difference between success and failure is often measured by your 'attitude' toward your set-backs.

Follow the example of Edison, don't give up after one or ten thousand failures. Use Edison's motivator—bulldog tenacity—to keep going onward and upward to success.


### INDIVIDUAL MOTIVATOR 5: *DYNAMIC FIRST IMPRESSIONS*

**ANDREW CARNEGIE USED THIS TECHNIQUE.** Andrew Carnegie, the steel magnate, used the art of *dynamic first impressions* to elevate himself to the top. Carnegie realized that whenever he was introduced to another he created a mental 'impression' of this person. Sometimes this initial impression turned out to be a wrong one after Carnegie got to 'really know' the individual. Carnegie reasoned that if his 'first impressions' could be wrong, the first impressions he himself presented could be misconstrued and hamper his chances of concluding favourable business transactions with others.

When you consider how you judge others when you first meet them you will see how you yourself are being judged. Your initial 'hello' can either help or hinder you, depending upon the 'impression' the other person forms of you. It might be the way you dress, the tone of your voice, the manner in which you express yourself, your views, your posture or any one of a hundred things the other person likes or dislikes.

Carnegie learned how to create *effective* first impressions. He used his creative intelligence to 'dress up' his image so that others were always impressed with his ability upon first meeting him. They wanted to meet this dynamic man again and to associate with him.


**FROM FACTORY BOY TO STEEL GIANT.** Carnegie began as a bobbin boy in a factory at little more than one dollar-a-week. He used an affirmative state of mind to impress others that he was capable of 'better things'. He subsequently moved ahead, becoming a telegraph messenger, a telegraph operator, an assistant to a railroad division-manager, then at the age of twenty four, the superintendent of the Western Division of the Pennsylvania Railroad Company.

From the humble beginnings of a dollar-a-week factory boy, Andrew Carnegie eventually gained controlling interest in a giant steel company. It has been estimated that Carnegie made in excess of $400 million in the production of steel.

**IT'S NOT HOW SMART YOU ARE—BUT HOW SMART OTHERS THINK YOU ARE THAT COUNTS.** Lawrence D. Brennan Ph.D., in his book **Make The Most of Your Hidden Mind Power*** states:

'It's not how smart you are, but how smart society thinks you are that counts. In a swift glance our mental worth is appraised. Whatever impression another gains of us will build an attitude that is difficult to change. Such attitudes can be changed if you take the right steps to change them. But it is easier and much better to concentrate on making good first impressions.'

**YOU ARE YOUR OWN WALKING ADVERTISEMENT.** Your personality is on display when you meet others for the first time and they immediately 'rate' you on your performance. Dynamic first impressions are an important success ingredient. You are your own 'best' or 'worst' walking advertisement.

Emulate Andrew Carnegie's individualized success technique— dynamic first impressions—by creating an *effective* greeting of your own. It should be warm, courteous and respectful of the other person's position in life.

**EMULATE THE QUALITIES OF THOSE YOU ADMIRE.** *People seldom improve, when they have no other model but themselves to copy after.*—GOLDSMITH.

Begin now, the habit of learning about success from others you admire. Select a successful individual in your community and arrange a social or business meeting. Ask questions concerning his or her success and write the answers in your note book. Study this person to find one or more personality traits you admire, then emulate them. Find out the 'success philosophy' and the 'motivator', jot them down and use them in your own life.

Devise your own 'individualized' motivators for success. Underscore the ones that appeal to you in this book then put them into practice *today*, for a successful *tomorrow*.

**SINGLE OUT A SUCCESSFUL HERO FROM HISTORY AND STUDY HIS CHARACTER.** In addition to singling out a successful individual who is associated with your work or who lives in your city or town, select a famous name from history. I have always admired the character traits of the late General Douglas MacArthur and Sir Winston Churchill. Both these 'men of history' had decisive minds and used them to become respected leaders. I endeavour to emulate their much admired affirmative qualities. Kids have their heroes. I see nothing wrong with adults having theirs.

---

*(Quest. Horwitz-Int. Inc.)

Practise the art of learning from others you respect. Select your own personal hero from history and emulate his character traits. Read every available piece of literature that has been written about your hero. Write the qualities you admire in your notebook. Picture in your mind's eye the strength of character and leadership qualities of your hero, then picture yourself in a prominent leadership role. As your affirmative consciousness pattern develops, you will gradually become 'that which you wish to be'.

**WHAT IS A LEADER?** 'Leadership is an elusive quality,' once remarked General Eisenhower. In terms of past and present individuals recognized to be strong leaders the following names come readily to mind: Napoleon, Wellington, George Washington, Winston Churchill, Douglas MacArthur, Konrad Adenauer and Charles de Gaulle, to mention a few. The leadership qualities exhibited by these men are attributes to be developed and practised if you want to be regarded as a self power and respected leader.

## 5 ESSENTIAL LEADERSHIP QUALITIES:

1. SELFLESS DEDICATION

2. COURAGE

3. CONVICTION

4. FORTITUDE

5. INTEGRITY

# SUMMARY OF IDEAS TO HELP
# YOU BECOME A SELF POWER

1. *Don't be frightened to confront prominent people. Ask them about their success. Listen carefully to their answers, write them down for future reference and application in your own life.*

2. *Apply motivators to help you succeed. Use the ones that appeal to you in this book or devise your own. 'Individualize' them to fit your specific needs. Here are the* **BIG 5** *INDIVIDUAL MOTIVATORS:*

   **POSITIVE ASSUMPTION**

   **VISUALIZATION**

   **AFFIRMATIVE REPETITION**

   **BULLDOG TENACITY**

   **DYNAMIC FIRST IMPRESSIONS**

3. *First impressions are important. You are your own 'best' or 'worst' walking advertisement. Create an effective 'hello'. Dress up your image so that others are impressed by you.*

4. *Select a hero from history and emulate his or her outstanding attributes. Picture in your mind's eye the strength of character and leadership qualities of your selected hero, then picture yourself as one possessing these desirable traits.*

# HOW TO APPLY THE *BIG 5 CHARACTER MOTIVATORS* THAT ELEVATE YOU TO THE TOP

SUCCESS
PRINCIPLE

**8**

# Success Ideas in this Chapter

*The noblest contribution which any man can make for the benefit of posterity, is that of a good character. The richest bequest which any man can leave to the youth of his native land, is that of a shining, spotless example.*

R. C WINTHROP

5 + 5 = SUCCESS. Motivators are essential ingredients for success. Your future happiness and prosperity can be programed with mathematical accuracy when you understand and apply powerful motivator principles.

The BIG 5 SUCCESS MOTIVATORS combined with the BIG 5 CHARACTER MOTIVATORS will help you to establish a success consciousness, develop leadership qualities and form character traits that others will admire and respect. You will be amazed at what motivators can do for you. Diligently apply them and you will begin to think faster, tackle problems with greater confidence, increase your happiness, health and your income.

**CHARACTER MOTIVATOR 1 : INTEGRITY.** There are no short cuts to success; success has a high price tag. The opportunities are there and the rewards are there but so are the demands.

To succeed it is necessary to 'get along' with people. It is also necessary to be working in a job you love and to have the knowledge to perform your work at top efficiency. Additionally, it is important that you become involved in every facet of your business. Success means hard work. You must be prepared to go the 'extra mile', to work in excess of a 40-hour week.

Success is earned. It is not 'charity' as any successful person will tell you. There is no such thing as 'something for nothing'. A lot of people believe this theory to hold true—it doesn't. Some people attempt to attain riches by devious methods. While dishonesty might seemingly work advantageously for some for a while, it can never bring lasting success. You achieve success through the diligent application of your talents in an honest and fair way. To do this is to show that you have a sense of integrity.

**INTEGRITY IS THE KEY TO A MAN'S CHARACTER.** To have the greatest character trait of all is to have integrity. It means that you can be trusted. It means that you can be counted on to come through in the clinches. It means you are honest in all of your dealings. It means that there is a purity and moral soundness about you as an individual.

Every employer wants to know that he is hiring individuals who are honest. If you cannot be trusted then you will never make it to the top. When others find that you lack integrity they will not deal with you. You can control the attitudes and actions of others only if they respect you. They respect you when they know you have personal integrity.

There is no substitute for integrity. It is the key to man's character and it is essential for success. Integrity, coupled with knowledge and desire, equals success. There is no use having all of the other attributes that make for success if you lack integrity, for sooner or later this 'lack' in your character will bring you to your knees and destroy all chance of 'greater things'.

Many people behave badly and make a mess of their lives because they lack integrity. They raise the hopes of others with promises they know they cannot keep. To do this, is inexcusable cruelty and gross dishonesty. The wise man is the man who realizes early in life that *honesty is the best policy*, that he can go far with personal integrity but nowhere without it. The successful man's destiny is determined by the degree of his integrity.

*Give us the man of integrity, on whom we know we can thoroughly depend; who will stand firm when others fail; the friend, faithful and true; the adviser, honest and fearless; the adversary, just and chivalrous; such a one is a fragment of the Rock of Ages.*—A. P. STANLEY.

**CHARACTER MOTIVATOR 2: FAITH.** There is no certain future for the individual who lacks faith; faith in himself; faith in others; faith in his community and faith in God. If external things can move you, you have no faith, for faith is like the Rock of Gibraltar—*unmovable*.

Faith is believing in the invisible forces of God. It is the inspiration that marches at the head of everything. It is the inspiration behind all great works of man. Faith is believing that 'works of good' will come to pass no matter what the obstacles.

When you believe that you are big enough to master any problem and have total faith in your own ability to win, success is not far off.

Set goals, *believe* in them and you will achieve them, for faith brings the visible out of the invisible.

Psychologist William James declared, 'There is but one cause of human failure and that is man's lack of faith in his true self.' Faith gives power and action to any desire you may have. The practise of faith in yourself, faith in others, faith in your community and faith in God, brings health, happiness and prosperity.

**FAITH SAVED TWO FROM DEATH IN THE YUKON.** As an example of *faith power*, examine the amazing story of Helen Klaben and Ralph Flores who spent 49 agonising days together on a mountainside in the Yukon—forty of them without food. Helen was twenty one and Flores forty two, when they met in Fairbanks, Alaska, early in 1963. Flores was seeking a passenger on a flight to California. Helen agreed to fly with him.

When their plane crashed into the trees near Aeroplane Lake, on the border of the Yukon Territory and British Columbia, experts gave them no more than a couple of days to survive in the frozen waste, where the temperature had dropped to around 50 degrees below zero. But the pair did survive because of a tremendous 'will to live' and a faith that was unbroken. 'I was determined to stick to my faith in my friend, God,' said Helen, in a newspaper account of their ordeal. 'I knew we would be rescued.'

Flores, a Morman lay minister, had implicit faith that rescue would come and that they would survive until rescued. Although a small man physically, Flores showed fantastic energy. He chopped down trees with a chisel and hammer and built fires for weeks when melted snow was their only sustenance which kept them alive until a plane spotted their SOS and they were rescued. *By grace are ye saved through faith; and that not of yourselves; it is the gift of God.* EPH. 2:8.

**FAITH MOVES MOUNTAINS.** Faith is an attitude of mind, a special way of thinking, a deep inner conviction. Faith or lack of it, is the deciding point between success or failure of any undertaking. Limitations and problems in your life indicate that you are lacking in strong belief; lacking in an affirmative attitude that 'turns the tables' on unfavourable circumstance and brings peace of mind, happiness and real joy.

The soundest wisdom to be found, is in that famous quotation which indicates that *faith moves mountains.* When you *really believe* and not just 'wish' or 'hope' for, your remove inner mountains of fear, frustration, tension and anxiety and leave the way clear for creative accomplishment. There's no use talking about success, hoping for it, dreaming of it, you have to apply real *faith* in your life and then, and *only* then, will you see your desires, dreams and aspirations bear fruit.

You are a product of your own belief. When you believe yourself to be 'inadequate' you are telling your subconscious mind that you are a failure. When you believe 'I can, I will', then 'you do'.

# APPLY FAITH IN 4 SIMPLE STEPS

*Step* 1: Think success and *believe* that you are capable of being successful. Cease to think in terms of what you cannot do, but in terms of what you *can* do. Never think failure. Failure is anti-faith.

*Step* 2: When opportunity appears, hold the deep conviction that, 'This is right for me. I will succeed.'

*Step* 3: Believe BIG. The size of your success is not determined by the size of your brain but by the size of your faith. Think BIG achievements and back them with BIG faith.

*Step* 4: Affirm this belief: '*Faith* is an attitude of mind. *Faith* is belief in myself, things, other people and God. I live in faith.'

**CHARACTER MOTIVATOR 3: ENTHUSIASM.** *Every great and commanding movement in the annals of the world is the triumph of enthusiasm. Nothing great was ever achieved without it.* This was the feeling of Ralph Waldo Emerson, poet and essayist; and how true. *Enthusiasm* is a magical word meaning *keen interest*. Lack of enthusiasm has kept many a man from achieving success.

Enthusiasm is the difference between caring and not caring, between interest and disinterest. Many stage performers I know captivate audiences by injecting great enthusiasm into everything they do. Wayne Newton is an example. On or off the stage, Wayne wins people with his infectious enthusiasm.

Enthusiasm is *energy motivated*. Energy is the capability for doing work. When a man works and plays he draws upon energy stored within his body. The degree to which he succeeds in his work is measured by the amount of energy he exerts.

The energy that makes organisations move, depends upon 'individual' enthusiasm. Leaders with bright ideas and the ability to inspire high thought and action in others are the main generators of energy. Their individual brand of enthusiasm rubs off onto other people and inspires them to greater works.

There are untapped sources of energy within all of us. When we tap our energy supply we become more dynamic, more productive and consequently more successful. Psychic energy combined with physical energy is a mighty power that can elevate your present position in life and bring your increased income through expanded personal production and creative accomplishment.

One of the things every potential leader must learn is how to get along with others in business and how to *motivate* them. The people being delegated duties must respect their leader. They must be 'impressed' with his special brand of enthusiasm and drive. What psychologists term 'psychological drive' is really another term for 'enthusiastic appeal' of an idea.

Lord Thomson, the British press tycoon, says that any young man who wishes to become a millionaire today must have a complete determination and be 'enthusiastic about his desire to be rich and successful'. Enthusiasm can be the turning point of any idea. Once a task is backed with enthusiasm, that task is half done.

**ENTHUSIASTIC PEOPLE HAVE NOTHING TO FEAR.** No person who is enthusiastic about his work, his friends, his family, has anything to fear from life. Opportunities are waiting to be grasped by people who are enthusiastic. Enthusiasm overcomes inertia, it dispels discouragement and loneliness. It draws 'good' to the person who displays it. *Love life* and it will love you back. Be *enthusiastic* about life and it will reward you with greater accomplishment.


# 5 ENTHUSIASM PICK-ME-UPS

Anyone can be enthusiastic when things are going well; it takes concentrated effort and courage to be enthusiastic when the going is tough. Here are five enthusiasm *pick-me-ups* to apply when things get you down.

**Pick-me-up 1**: When you feel depressed because of negative circumstance and your thoughts are negative, *reverse* them and project thoughts of what you most want to happen in your life. Experience *now* the happiness, love, peace and joy you desire. Jump up, shout it to the roof tops and pour *enthusiasm* into your desire for a happier life. This sudden rush of energy will dissolve your mental inertia and feelings of depression.

**Pick-me-up 2**: If you desire more friends, if you want more people to be around you, to admire you and to love you, then the very next person you speak to, greet with *enthusiasm*. Show to others the admiration and love you seek.

**Pick-me-up 3**: Act like an enthusiastic person. *Get on fire*. Project a sparkling personality that marks you as a dynamic person. Act enthusiastically toward everything and you'll be marked as an enthusiastic person.

**Pick-me-up** 4: Lethargy pyramids, so does enthusiasm. Don't be lethargic in the morning, enthusiastic at noon and lethargic again in the evening. Jump out of bed in the morning with enthusiasm for 'what's ahead' and stay that way until you retire.

**Pick-me-up** 5: Associate with enthusiastic people. They'll influence your life in like manner. Enthusiastic people are the *now* people. They are cheerful, happy, zestful. Enthusiastic people will inspire you to achieve greater things in life. Make friends with enthusiastic people. They are excellent mental pick-me-ups. When you are around them their enthusiasm won't allow for loneliness or fits of depression.

**CHARACTER MOTIVATOR 4: DISCIPLINE.** Discipline is a most important character trait to possess. Individuals need it as well as nations. Without discipline the world would totter. During the second World War, England could not have survived the daily bombings without the individual discipline of its people. Londoners went to the shelters at night, not knowing whether their homes would still be standing in the morning. But yet, they kept on living. This is discipline. No army could march unless it was under discipline. No company could operate successfully unless it's staff was under discipline. With discipline comes organization, strength of purpose, determination and success. Without discipline there is disorganization, confusion and failure.

**DO ONE THING AT A TIME.** Some people cannot seem to accomplish anything. They work on many projects but all seem to falter and fail. This is because they do not tackle one job at a time and see it through. This is lack of discipline.

The completion of a goal brings happiness. Accomplishment brings confidence to tackle something bigger, something better. The people who accomplish many things and reap success after success are those who tackle *one job at a time*, complete it, then move on to the next. This is *organization*; this is *discipline*.

Get your life organized in such a way that your time is used to the best advantage. Do the important jobs now, the trivial things can wait. Carry each job through to completion. To do this is to avoid confusion. Back your organized effort with enthusiasm, faith and integrity. You will accomplish your goals twice as fast and you will be establishing a success pattern for future goals. Do one thing at a time and *do it right*.

**YOU CAN SUCCEED AS MANY TIMES AS YOU MAKE UP YOUR MIND TO SUCCEED.** Each job or experience is a necessary 'lesson in life' from which knowledge is gained to be used in the successful completion of further aims. Initially, you may incur one success and twenty failures. Discipline your mind to dwell on the success, not on the failures. Focus your full attention on your proven accomplishment. That's one; more will follow. If you succeed once, you can succeed twice and a third and fourth time or as many times as you set your mind to it.


**DISCIPLINE THE EMOTIONS.** Without emotions, life would not be worth living. Through our various emotions we 'experience' things. When our emotions are of an affirmative nature we experience affirmative living. When our emotions are negative, we tend to be unhappy, unhealthy, lonely, frustrated, fearful and virtually living within a state of 'hell on earth'. Emotions can be controlled. They can be disciplined to react affirmatively, thereby creating health, joy, love, peace of mind, confidence, etc. Affirmative emotions create a 'heaven on earth' environment.

Control your life by controlling your emotions. Discipline your mind to harbour only affirmative thoughts which create an affirmative consciousness pattern, which in turn, creates well being and harmonious living conditions.


**PATIENCE IS A VIRTUE.** To be successful requires a certain degree of patience. 'To know how to wait is the great secret of success,' said Joseph De Maistre, the Sardinian writer. Everything cannot come at once. To climb a mountain takes courage, stamina, discipline, faith and patience. So it is with success. Lack of patience indicates a lack of discipline which is a definite handicap. For those who seek success, impatience creates obstacles and needless delays. The quickest way to the top is the *direct* approach. Stopping, starting, being diverted, becoming impatient, is *indirect* and the least successful means of accomplishment. If things are not progressing as quickly as you might want, be patient. *Nothing moves but by degrees.* Each step forward, no matter how small, is one step less that has to be taken.

Learn the art of patience. Apply discipline to your thoughts when they become anxious over the outcome of a goal. Impatience breeds anxiety, fear, discouragement and failure. Patience creates confidence, decisiveness and a rational outlook, which eventually leads to success. *Everything comes if a man will only wait.*—TANCRED.

# HOW TO EFFECT DISCIPLINE
# IN YOUR LIFE

**Step 1:** Control your emotions by disciplining your thoughts. Project *affirmative thoughts* when fear arises over the outcome of any project. Reverse negative thoughts immediately. Affirmative thoughts constitute controlled emotions.

**Step 2:** Be patient. Impatience is a sign of immaturity. You would not dig up seeds to see whether they were growing. Cultivate ideas and desires, execute them and patiently await the fruits of your labour.

**Step 3:** Work out a step-by-step plan for each goal. Take one project at a time and complete it. You can only move effectively in one direction at one time. You can think only one thought at a time. Don't take on too much at once. Discipline yourself to the accomplishment of one task before moving on to the next.

**Step 4:** Keep a written record of your goals, and of your progress. Whatever needs to be done, do it. Don't put off the important things to fiddle with trivialities. Discipline yourself to *get the job done* in the shortest possible time. If you have to write an article, a book, prepare a speech, a sermon, dig the garden, paint the house, sell the car, call on a tough prospect, *do it*.

**CHARACTER MOTIVATOR 5: APPRECIATION.** You should never condemn anything. To condemn something is to negate consciously, and anything you negate has a habit of finding its way back to you in some identical form. *Watch your words.* Words of 'good', are energized and vitalized, they grow and bring forth after their kind.

Give genuine appreciation for life around you. Give thanks for the daily pleasures you experience in your life; for the joys to be found in music, art and literature. Give thanks for the work you are employed in and for the ability to carry it out. Give thanks for your family and friends without whom life would be less enjoyable. Show appreciation of the natural and beautiful things: mountains, lakes, trees, flowers, the birds and animals. To do this is to *appreciate* life and to partake of its pleasures.

Fill your home with appreciation. Never make an assertion in your home that you would not like to see continue. When you talk poverty and lack, you are opening the doors to these unwelcome states and inviting them into your life. Express affirmative thoughts of love, health, joy, prosperity and appreciation for all that you possess. Never say money is scarce, or things are difficult. *Talk* prosperity, *think* prosperity and give *thanks* for prosperity in your life.

**IF YOU WANT TO SUCCEED, LEARN TO APPRECIATE OTHERS.** On many occasions, success depends on the support you receive from other people. It often happens that the only 'obstacle' in your way is another person or other persons. Therefore, it is necessary to cultivate the habit of *appreciation* of others. Everyone likes to be appreciated. This is a common fact of human relations. Everyone from the cradle to the rocking chair desires admiration, appreciation and respect.

If you wish to succeed in any endeavour you have to learn to like people, appreciate their individual talents and tell them so. This does not mean insincere flattery for the purpose of winning points. Insincerity is for the phoney. The phoney seldom succeeds.

**EVERYONE NEEDS SOMEONE.** Everyone needs the support and confidence of someone. The salesman needs a buyer for his merchandise. If the salesman cannot gain the support of others for his goods, he fails as a salesman. The executive depends on the support of his staff to get things done. Without their support, he fails as an executive. The politician requires the support of his constituents. Without their support he cannot be elected.

**BOB HOPE KNOWS THE VALUE OF APPRECIATION.** Bob Hope appreciates the abilities of his aides and they in turn show him loyalty and affection. Hope's agent has been with him for more than 30 years. His public relations man about 20 years and his office staff for long stretches as well. He appreciates them and they respond with loyalty.

**HOW TO GET OTHERS TO SUPPORT YOU.** The way to get the support of other people is very simple: *apprèciate them and tell them so.* If you wanted a particular individual to do you a favour you would not demand or physically force him to do it. For obvious reasons this approach wouldn't work. When others feel that you genuinely admire, respect and appreciate them, they'll help you to 'move mountains'.

**THE SECRET NEED OF ALL OF US.** Every human being, regardless of origin, has one basic desire: *to feel important and to command the respect of others.* This point is worth remembering. Each human being, whether he lives in Australia or Zambia, wants to be liked and wants to feel important.

Whenever dealing with other people, always keep in mind that 'to be appreciated' is man's strongest desire. To know this and to do something about it will take you far in your personal and business dealings with others.

Make other people feel important by remembering their names, by addressing them in a respectful manner and by asking their advice on matters they are expert on. Compliment others on their dress, their manner, the efficient way they work. By appreciating them, they'll appreciate you.

*He is incapable of truly good action who finds not a pleasure in contemplating the good actions of others.*—LAVATER

# 10 WAYS TO APPRECIATE OTHERS TO HAVE THEM APPRECIATE YOU

1. Practise appreciation. Show others you like them. Start with your wife, your family, your friends. Compliment a hairstyle, a dress or suit, a newly acquired possession, a garden, *anything* that deserves a compliment. Watch a smile and pleasant response come from the person being complimented. *Do it sincerely.* Others know when you sincerely like them. They also know when you are insincerely flattering them. They 'feel' it by means of vibration.

2. Make the other person *feel important.* If there is a subject or a problem that another can help you with, make the approach this way: 'You are regarded as an authority on this matter. I wonder if you would be kind enough to assist me.' Pat the other fellow on the back. Elevate his position in life. Make him feel he is important. Give sincere thanks for his help.

3. Never criticize without complimenting. No one likes to be told they are inadequate in their job. Criticize constructively, then praise at least one attribute.

4. Always greet people with a sincere smile. Human beings react to the attitude *behind* your greeting. Greet them enthusiastically, be genuinely pleased to see them.

5. When in the company of others never gossip or negate the ability or personality of another. If you can't say anything pleasant about someone *don't say anything.*

6. Remember people's names. Pronounce the name correctly and always add the appropriate title such as: Mr, Mrs, Miss, Dr, Professor, Sir, etc. Titles make people feel important, *use them.*

7. When in conversation with others, don't hog the spotlight. A good conversationalist is popular, a good listener even more so. Talk if you have something to say, but *listen* and show interest in what others have to say.

8. Always be willing to help another; be it advice or the right word in the right direction at the right time. When you assist someone else up the success ladder, he or she may be in a position to help you at some future time.

9. Show your appreciation of another's efforts on your behalf by personally thanking or sending a note of 'thanks'. Little courtesies reap big dividends.

10. In appreciating others talents be tolerant of those who do not measure up to your standards. *No one is perfect.*

# SUMMARY OF IDEAS TO GET
# YOU TO THE TOP

1. *There are no short cuts to success. Success has a high price tag. The rewards are there for those who are prepared to* **work hard** *and* **honestly.**

2. *The noblest contribution which any man can make is that of a good character. Develop a strong character by applying the* **BIG 5** CHARACTER MOTIVATORS. They are:

    **INTEGRITY**

    **FAITH**

    **ENTHUSIASM**

    **DISCIPLINE**

    **APPRECIATION**

3. *Learn to* **like** *and* **appreciate** *others. Everyone needs someone to succeed. The salesman needs the buyer, the executive a loyal conscientious staff, the politician his constituents. Cultivate friends and associates by showing them that you like them and by recognizing their importance.*

4. *Never criticize without complimenting. No one likes to be torn down.*

5. *When others help you, thank them personally or by sending them a note of thanks.*

# HOW TO REAP A GOLDEN HARVEST OF RICHES FROM THE ACTION PLAN

## Success Ideas in this Chapter

- If You Want To Succeed Be Explicit About What You Want
- Few Bargains At The Success Counter
- A Plan Of Action Made His First Million
- Don't Wander Aimlessly
- The First Step To Successful Living
- Mother Of Two Children Earned High Degree
- Hubert Humphrey's Action Plan
- Plans Are Guide Posts To Success
- Burning Desire Brings Success
- The ACTION Plan
- A Guide To Help You Plan Goals
- Tackle One Thing At A Time
- If You Want To Succeed Find A Strong Incentive
- Ideas Are The Beginning Of Everything
- The Power Of Lenin's Ideas
- The Power Of Hitler's Ideas
- $1 Million A Year For Workable Ideas
- SIMPLE Ideas Create Fortunes
- Helena Rubinstein Made Millions From An Idea Started in Melbourne
- Howard Hughes Devised The Electric Bed While Lying Ill In Hospital
- Wanted—Imagination
- Talents And Ideas Need Presentation
- Sell Yourself Professionally: The Resumé–The Biography–The Covering Letter–The Interview
- 4 Helpful Pointers
- Some Do's And Don'ts
- Attention To Dress And Manners: For The Man—For The Woman
- Summary Of Ideas To Reap A Golden Harvest Of Riches

*The method of the enterprising is to plan with audacity, and execute with vigor; to sketch out a map of possibilities, and then to treat them as probabilities.*

BOVEE

---

**IF YOU WANT TO SUCCEED BE EXPLICIT ABOUT WHAT YOU WANT.** Ask a youngster what he'd like to become in life and you will receive a decisive answer. He will tell you he wants to be an astronaut, a jet pilot, a doctor, an actor or a soldier. Children are affirmative in their wants—perhaps a little unrealistic but seldom indefinite or non-committal. Ask an adult what it is he or she desires in life and more often than not the answer will be anything but specific.

What do *you* want in life? Do you know? Could you clearly define your goals at this very moment?

To experience success it is necessary to know precisely what it is you want and to draft suitable plans for the accomplishment of your desires. Write them down; be explicit. Know exactly what you wish to make of your life, the things you want to accomplish : perfect health, successful marriage, peace of mind, a new job, a new house, a trip abroad, a specific amount of money or what? No matter what it is you desire in life you can achieve it if you focus your thoughts upon your objective and *plan* for it. In this vast world there is an answer to every need, an opportunity to experience health, happiness and prosperity. God supplies you with the necessary equipment to succeed but you have to supply the goods and the *will* to win. *For every one that asketh receiveth; and he that seeketh findeth; and to him that knocketh it shall be opened.*—LUKE 11:10.

When you know what you want and have a clear cut *plan of action*

121

you are able to embrace the future with joyful anticipation instead of clinging to past fruitless dreams and wishes that manifest failure. Planned goals are dreams being acted upon; they keep you moving ahead in life.

**FEW BARGAINS AT THE SUCCESS COUNTER.** There is a price men must pay to achieve success and the price is never cheap. There are few bargains at the success counter. Success is earned by those who know what they want, have a definite plan of action and are willing to work hard to accomplish their goals.

Although many people desire to be successful, few are willing to make the sacrifices that are necessary to the accomplishment of high aims. They lack knowledge, preparation and the ability to 'stick it out' when conditions are less than favourable.

**A PLAN OF ACTION MADE HIS FIRST MILLION.** London newspapers reported the story of an enterprising young man who, seven years after leaving school, at the age of twenty three, made his first million. Barry Rowe, the son of a London scrap metal merchant, is now well on the way to making his second million dollars.

'I made this large amount by buying up old houses, doing them up and selling them at a profit. I had no help. I just had ideas, a plan and a desire to make money, so I borrowed from the bank and bought some old properties,' Barry told astounded London journalists.

**DON'T WANDER AIMLESSLY.** Show me an individual wandering aimlessly through life without a definite plan of action to achieve desired goals and I'll show you a failure. Life itself has a plan and it works according to set principles. So must *you* have a plan so that you know where you are headed.

You would not think of commencing a long automobile journey without a map or knowing in which direction to proceed. If, for example, you wanted to drive in a northerly direction and you took off in the direction that was due south, your chance of reaching your desired destination would be slim.

Life's journey is infinitely more important than an automobile trip, yet, astonishingly enough, many people spend more time mapping out their summer vacation than they spend planning their future. To wander aimlessly through life without a plan, not knowing where you are headed or why, is sheer folly.

Don't waste your time the way some people spend their money. Search for the reasons 'why' you are, where you are. Are you experiencing failure because of vague ideas about desired goals? Are you wasting valuable years wandering through life not knowing where you are headed?

**THE FIRST STEP TO SUCCESSFUL LIVING.** There was a period of my life in Canada, when I yearned to become a successful stage and television performer. At the time I was publishing a number of successful newspapers and had it not been for a strong desire to succeed in another profession, in all likelihood, I would still be a newspaper publisher.

In addition to the long hours needed to operate the newspapers, I was rushing around attempting to fulfil lecture commitments and working long into the night to churn out scripts for three weekly drama and musical programs my radio and television packaging company was producing. Having a great deal to do and little time in which to do it, brought anxiety, frustration and eventually an ulcer. Although successful in one sphere of endeavour, I was still unhappy in the knowledge that my real desire—to be a successful performer—was nowhere near realization.

I decided to implement a five-year plan of action that would eventually see me clear of my Canadian interests and free to take up permanent residence in Hollywood, where I could devote full time and interest to my goals. My plan of action was set out in five one-year periods. The first period was set aside for study, the second period for study and securing a U.S. visa. The third period for securing an agent and manager and for the disposal of my Canadian interests and so on.

Once the plan was underway, I noticed a remarkable change in my physical health. The ulcer disappeared when feelings of fear, tension, anxiety and frustration dissolved. I now had a *definite* mission—to succeed as a performer—and a clear cut plan of action to achieve it. I also found that my other work became a lot easier. I accomplished things in far less time and with fewer anxious moments. I was enthusiastic about my life and happy in the knowledge that at last I was headed in the direction I desired.


**MOTHER OF TWO CHILDREN EARNED HIGH DEGREE.** Recently a Sydney newspaper published the story of a mother of two children who went to university and earned a doctorate in Philosophy, one of the highest university degrees.

The woman explained to the press that for her, going to university was an ambition seeking an outlet. 'I was bored, so I did something about it,' she said.

Comedian Bob Hope is often quoted as saying: 'You've got to keep moving or you're not living.' Those who know what they want and have a plan to achieve it, are enthusiastic and happy people because they are constantly moving ahead and *experiencing* the fruits of their labours. They succeed more times than fail because life for them is definite.

**HUBERT HUMPHREY'S ACTION PLAN.** In 1935 when Hubert Humphrey was twenty four and a scout leader in Huron, South Dakota, he took his troop on a trip to Washington. Sitting in his hotel room Hubert Humphrey decided he would one day live in Washington and become a member of Congress. In a letter to his fiancee, Muriel Buck, Hubert wrote that he intended to set a plan of action to reach his goal. He cautioned her not to laugh at his high aim: 'Others have done it and if you and I apply ourselves to make up our minds to work for bigger things we can live here in Washington and be in Government service,' he wrote.

Hubert Humphrey's 'plan of action' took him up the political ladder to the number two position in the U.S. Government as Vice President and the chance to contest the top position in the 1968 Presidential elections.


**PLANS ARE GUIDE POSTS TO SUCCESS.** Success arrives by design; failure by the lack of it. Plans are the guide posts along life's road to success; without them the road is an unsure and rocky one. Poorly devised plans will never harvest riches. Achievements can be no greater than the undertakings. If your plans are sketchy and your aims low, you can never hope to achieve high rewards. When you pursue goals in a scientific way you succeed more times than fail.

Visualize the goals you wish to accomplish. Actually see yourself receiving a job promotion, being given a raise in salary, selling your automobile, taking that long dreamed-of overseas trip or being handed the key to your dream home. Know that a well laid out plan of action coupled with an affirmative consciousness pattern will bring the life you seek.


**BURNING DESIRE BRINGS SUCCESS.** A famous movie actress told me in Hollywood, that as a young girl she carried a burning desire to be a movie star. 'I used to see my name in lights. I even constructed a model theatre from cardboard and painted my name on the marquee. My plan was to study drama, move to Hollywood and become a star.' Then she added, 'I still have that model theatre I built twenty years ago and I can't help feeling that the mental pictures I held of myself as a star and my plans to achieve becoming one are the real reasons behind my success.'


**THE ACTION PLAN.** To see where you are going in life it is best to begin by drafting a *master plan* or an overall *pattern* covering your entire life span then reducing it to single short-term aims. Follow THE ACTION PLAN idea presented in this chapter by outlining *specifically* your objectives in life.

# A GUIDE TO HELP YOU PLAN GOALS

1. Increase in income.

2. Different job or profession.

3. Additional schooling.

4. A new house, automobile or boat.

5. An overseas trip.

6. Additional funds for future schooling of children.

7. New friends.

8. A wife or husband.

9. Overcome an illness.

10. Acquire social status in the community.

11. Acquire leadership positions in the community.

12. Develop and exploit specific creative talents: art, music, literary abilities, etc.

**(A) DESIRED GOALS:** Do first things first—*plan*. When building a house you don't buy the light fixtures first, you purchase the bricks and cement. What is it you want? Write down your goals in terms of their value and your attitudes and beliefs toward them. Write them down in detail. List short-term goals—those to be accomplished under one year—and long-term objectives—five years or more.

**(B) THE ACTION GROUP:** Success requires the assistance of others. You cannot do it all alone. Carefully select a *master mind* group who will be the honorary board of directors of your corporation—SELF.

You are in the business of life to *succeed* not to fail and you *can* succeed by applying your own creative talents and enlisting the experienced services of others.

The group you gather around you may differ slightly to the one shown in the Action Plan, depending of course, upon your aims. Your action group should consist of trusted, experienced and loyal individuals. They form a valuable link in your success chain.

1. **Accountant:** A qualified accountant familiar with every facet of taxation is one of the most important associates you will need. An experienced accountant can save you money in matters of personal tax and investment.

2. **Banker:** Select a bank of your choice and get on friendly terms with the manager. Make regular deposits each week no matter how small. This indicates that you are a conscientious saver. A friendly bank manager is your direct source to required funds for business or personal expansion.

3. **Insurance Agent:** Insurance is a source of security and investment. Seek a qualified insurance agent and get to know him on friendly terms.

4. **Realtor:** Real estate investments have made millionaires out of those who saw 'potential' and gambled on winning. Undeveloped land, apartment blocks, homes, can be profitable investments. A realtor is in the 'know' of what property is being offered and it's potential investment return.

5. **Stock Broker:** If you hanker to play the stock market, you will need *expert* advice on which stocks to buy, which stocks to stay clear of and *when* to sell. The uninformed run the risk of loss in the stock market gamble.

6. **Legal Adviser:** A competent and thoroughly reliable legal man is the best investment you could make. Seek one by means of recommendation. You will need contracts read and legal advice on personal as well as business matters.

**7. Medical Practitioner:** You cannot perform if you are constantly experiencing ill-health. There is a reason for aches and pains and stomach disorders. Nervous tension leads to ulcers, heart attacks and other illnesses. Get a regular check-up. Feel secure in the knowledge that you are physically well and able to mentally cope with problems as they arise.

**8. Religious Confidant:** Regularly attend a church of your choice. Make the personal acquaintance of the minister, priest or rabbi. In times of need, spiritual advice can be the turning point of the problem at hand and supply you with the comfort and support you need.

**9. Personal Confidant:** Everyone should have at least one loyal friend. Loyal friends are always ready to lend a helping hand during an emergency.

**10. Business Confidant:** Strike up a relationship with a fellow businessman in your office or in a company you deal with. Someone who is in an allied field to your own can often supply leads and business advice.

**(C) PLAN OF ACTION:** Your goal-striving effectiveness is enhanced when you know *how* you intend to win success. In order to get the feeling that you are accomplishing something, that there is 'hope' for better things, a definite plan of action is required. How do you intend going about accomplishing the goals you have set? A specific plan is like a road map—it shows you how to reach your final destination. It gives you confidence. You *know* where you are headed. When you are able to tick off each success as it arrives, you automatically build a reservoir of confidence to help you to accomplish your next goal. It is much like following your road map—as you pass through each town on the way, you confidently drive on, knowing that eventually you will arrive at your final destination.

You will need to draft your plans in exactly the same manner as any large company plans its progress:

PRODUCTION PLANS

MERCHANDISING PLANS

FINANCIAL PLANS

PROGRESS REPORTS

Place a tentative completion date alongside each goal. Have some idea in your mind how long each goal should take to accomplish. Set a date and work toward it. Be *specific* as to your plan of attack. Map out

# THE ACTION PLAN

(A) GOALS

1. ————————————————————————————————

2. ————————————————————————————————

3. ————————————————————————————————

4. ————————————————————————————————

5. ————————————————————————————————


(B) ACTION GROUP

1. Accountant: —————————————————————

2. Banker: ——————————————————————————

3. Insurance Agent: ———————————————————

4. Realtor: —————————————————————————

5. Stock Broker: ————————————————————

6. Legal Adviser: ——————————————————

7. Medical Practioner: ———————————————

8. Religious Confidant: ——————————————

9. Personal Confidant: (Husband–Wife–Friend): ———

10. Business Confidant: ——————————————— ————

(C) PLAN OF ACTION

Goal 1: ———————————————————————

Goal 2: ———————————————————————

Goal 3: ———————————————————————

Goal 4: ———————————————————————

Goal 5: ———————————————————————

(D) PROGRESS REPORT ———————————————————

Goal 1: ———————————————————————

Goal 2: ———————————————————————

Goal 3: ———————————————————————

Goal 4: ———————————————————————

Goal 5: ———————————————————————

(E) GOALS ACHIEVED

1. ——————————————————— ☐

2. ——————————————————— ☐

3. ——————————————————— ☐

4. ——————————————————— ☐

5. ——————————————————— ☐

your direction as carefully as you would a long distance journey. Keep large goals as part of a long term plan, smaller goals as part of a short term plan. Be realistic. There's no sense planning to become a state senator in three months. That's a long term goal. Becoming a member of the executive of an association or club to which you belong is a short term goal. Building a house might be a long term goal depending upon your immediate financial position. Buying a new automobile might be a short term goal.

Keep asking yourself 'HOW?' you intend to achieve each goal until a definite plan of action formulates. Definite well-laid plans are your insurance against failure. Be encouraged by them. Look at them and know that they are a sound investment in your own corporation — SELF.

**(D) PROGRESS REPORT:** Keep a written progress report on your journey to success. Draw a graph and watch it rise. Don't be discouraged if you should experience set-backs; ride with them. Failure is temporary and there is always an equivalent success waiting around the next corner. *Everything goes in cycles.* Be encouraged by knowing that your abilities and personality are unique and you have unlimited possibilities for growth and success.

When set-backs occur, check your plan of action. Do you have sufficient background material at hand? Enough experience as yet? Are you going about things in the wrong manner? Are you expecting too much, too soon? Some people expect and demand too much of themselves. Be patient if things do not seem to be progressing as rapidly as you want. Attempting to force a positive result to any situation is unwise and usually ends in failure. *Self control* is a necessary ingredient in your make up if you wish to succeed. Don't push *too* hard; don't break your head against the wall of life. Move ahead one step at a time.

**(E) GOALS ACHIEVED:** As you achieve each desired goal, check it off on your master plan. Perhaps you will go beyond your expectations and achieve other successes. Write them in the *Goals Achieved* column. They will give you ideas for further triumphs. Each goal achieved is encouragement to tackle something bigger and better.

**TACKLE ONE THING AT A TIME.** Many people try to accomplish too many things at one time. This only leads to confusion and frustration. Jumping from one thing to the next is a sign of an immature and disorganized mind. It also indicates a lack of discipline on the part of those who practise it.

Organize your day by preparing a schedule of events. Divide your day into parts. Within each 24-hour period devote eight hours to your job, eight hours to the pursuit of knowledge, entertainment and recreation and eight hours to sleep. Don't leave yourself a mental and physical wreck by attempting to do too much at any one time. We often inflict great physical and mental punishment upon ourselves in the pursuit of success; it seldom pays dividends.

Harness enthusiasm for *one* job and put all your energies into the accomplishment of that job. You will accomplish your desire twice as fast and you will avoid confusion. The people with dynamic personalities are the ones who have orderly thoughts. They concentrate on one thing at a time and go after it.

**IF YOU WANT TO SUCCEED FIND A STRONG INCENTIVE.** When your goals are clear and you accept their importance, it is necessary for you to then apply *all* your energy toward their fulfilment —*to finish what you start.* A strong *incentive* is essential in this case. Feel that your goals are worthwhile. Make certain that they are clear in your mind. If you attempt a plan of action which is not clear to you, confusion will reign and you will lose incentive. If you lack incentive or do not feel the importance of your plan, loss of interest will lead to subsequent failure.

Failure exists in this world because the student or worker does not have sufficient incentive to succeed nor the vision of what education and proper planning can accomplish. Everything that you do must have *meaning.* It must mean something to you *personally.* Unless you *really* want to accomplish a goal you won't. There has to be a real reason *why* you want something and it should be a sufficiently strong reason—*the incentive*—if you wish it to materialize in your life.

**IDEAS ARE THE BEGINNING OF EVERYTHING.** All things begin with an idea; you rise in the morning, make decisions, partake of food, drive your automobile, buy and sell merchandise, read the paper, all because of specific ideas which form in your mind. Your entire life is governed by your ideas. Your ideas are living 'things' that either make you happy or unhappy, healthy or ill, successful or unsuccessful.

The ideas you create in your conscious mind and pass along to your subconscious will eventually manifest themselves as outer circumstances. Put belief, feeling and enthusiasm behind your ideas and they will come to pass. This is how you become what you wish to become, how you achieve what you desire to achieve. This is how you succeed, instead of fail. Back ideas with faith and they will shape your destiny in an affirmative way.

**THE POWER OF LENIN'S IDEAS.** The enormity of ideas can be related to the Communist Empire, which little more than half a century ago measured an area of only two square feet. This was inside a restaurant in Zurich, where Nikolai Lenin, seated at a coffee table, shaped his ideas. Leninism came about in Russia following the revolution in 1917. Today, a mere handful of men virtually dominate all of Eastern Europe and Southern Asia. More than one billion people are enslaved because of one man's specific 'idea' of a political and social system of Government.

THE POWER OF HITLER'S IDEAS. Adolph Hitler founded the National Socialist Party with a single idea and the assistance of seven crackpots in the backroom of a beerhall. Hitlerism brought destruction, ruin and misery to the world during the twelve years this despot clung to his idea of world domination by militarism.

*Ideas* count; *ideas* change destiny; *ideas* create success or failure depending upon their worthiness. Hitler failed because his ideas were evil. *Like attracts like.* Evil ideas produce after their own kind. If Hitler had realized the significance of the following Bible truth he might not have drawn the world into war: *Be not deceived; God is not mocked; for whatsoever a man soweth, that shall he also reap.—* GALATIONS 6:7.

$1 MILLION A YEAR FOR WORKABLE IDEAS. The Ford Motor Company in Dearborne, Michigan, pays $1 million a year for constructive ideas submitted by its employees. If you have a bright idea on how to save Ford production costs and enhance their products, send it to them, it could be worth money to you if they accept it.

In excess of $15 million is paid out every year by American industry to 'Mr Average', for bright ideas. Get cracking, your idea, if it is workable, is worth money. Develop it, believe in it, then sell it.

SIMPLE IDEAS CREATE FORTUNES. Ideas do not have to be involved to make millions. The bobbypin is an example of a simple, yet widely used aid that brought a fortune to its inventor. The safety pin, corkscrew, can opener and the paper clip, are a few others that brought high rewards to their creators.

When an idea comes to mind, write it down, think about it, enlarge upon it, become enthusiastic about it, then do something about it. An idea rattling around in your head will bring you little more than a headache. Ideas have to be nurtured, their potential developed, then action taken to bring them to reality. It is like planting a seed; nature takes it up and something evolves. So it is with ideas. The thought is the seed, the subconscious takes it up and something evolves it and makes it manifest as circumstance.

A bright idea could be the turning point of your life if you *follow through*, as did Walt Disney, when he discovered a new method of animation after reading about the subject in a library book.

**HELENA RUBINSTEIN MADE MILLIONS FROM AN IDEA STARTED IN MELBOURNE.** Helena Rubinstein, the cosmetics manufacturer who died at ninety four, left an estate valued in excess of $34 million. The beauty queen started her vast cosmetics empire with an idea, a jar of cold cream and a small rented room in Collins Street, Melbourne.

Mme Rubinstein arrived in Australia at the age of twenty one, bringing with her a cold cream prepared by a chemist in her home town of Cracow in Poland. When great numbers of women commented on her soft, creamy complexion, she decided to import the cream. It sold so readily that she bought the formula and with a small amount of capital set up the Helena Rubinstein Beauty Salon. From these beginnings the business flourished and spread to Paris, London, New York and a hundred other cities around the world.

**HOWARD HUGHES DEVISED THE ELECTRIC BED WHILE LYING ILL IN HOSPITAL.** In 1946 multi-millionaire Howard Hughes was nearly killed while test-flying an experimental plane that crashed on its maiden flight. Hughes showed inventive skill while lying ill in the hospital by designing a bed operated by 30 electric motors. Push buttons allowed him to adjust the bed to various positions to ease the pain. Instead of lying helpless, Hughes used his thinking powers to produce a workable and highly rewarding invention.

**WANTED!—IMAGINATION.** Where do you find ideas? How do you think them up? Everything comes out of the *invisible*; that's where ideas are. The notion that there is 'nothing new under the sun', is a false one. New things are being discovered every day. Ideas in plentiful supply are housed in the Universal Mind, waiting to be expressed.

Here's how you can discover and develop ideas:

1. OBSERVE.

2. INQUIRE.

3. QUESTION.

4. THINK.

5. LOOK AT A COMMON PROBLEM AND TRY TO SOLVE IT. (Ideas spring from problems)

6. READ PUBLICATIONS THAT PRESENT NEW IDEAS AND DEVELOPMENTS.

7. DISCUSS IDEAS WITH OTHERS.

8. WRITE DOWN EVERY IDEA THAT COMES TO MIND AND ENLARGE ON IT.

Ideas need not be complex to be valuable, nor do you have to be a genius to discover and develop worthy ideas. A housewife, banker, nurse, boilermaker, executive or student can develop saleable ideas as readily as a scientist.

Ideas often present themselves at odd moments. They could come while reading the morning newspaper, while taking a walk, doing your shopping, watching a film in a theatre, sitting in front of the television set or listening to a commentator on the radio. Many times they present themselves while lying awake in bed. Always keep a pencil and paper handy so you can jot them down immediately they 'pop' into your consciousness.

Other 'idea' sources are: libraries, trade papers, Government sources, local, national and international newspapers and magazines. Ideas come from many sources. It takes only one *good* idea successfully promoted to reap a golden harvest of riches.

TALENTS AND IDEAS NEED PRESENTATION. When I completed school, I went to work for an advertising agency in Sydney as a copywriter. I never ceased to be amazed at the slick presentation material the agency produced when attempting to sign up a new account.

Firstly, the copywriters supplied the art department with a rough presentation layout which they in turn worked on to design a colourful presentation folder. It looked thoroughly professional. It was neat, precise, appealing and put forth a definite point of view aimed at impressing the prospective client on the ability of the agency to mount a successful advertising program for him.

I have used a portfolio presentation to enhance my own career. While in New York, I had an advertising agency make up a presentation folder based on how I wished to be 'sold' to producers. The brochures have always brought a favourable response from producers and agents and have helped me to gain a great deal of theatrical employment.

SELL YOURSELF PROFESSIONALLY. Organize your own product presentation whether it is a simple folder that includes a biography and resume or an elaborate brochure on your merchandise, product, company or store. Make it colourful and make it to the point. It should motivate others to want to hire you or purchase the goods you have to sell.

THE RESUMÉ: Employers are favourably impressed when they receive a well laid out resumé. Have it professionally typed and copied. Place it in a neat, plain (not coloured) folder. Always include a covering letter when mailing your application for a position. Type it and sign it with a legible signature. Your resume should include the following information:

1. Name, address and telephone number.
2. Age, marital status.
3. Schooling.
4. Previous positions held (leave no historical gaps).
5. Appraise your qualifications and note them briefly.

**THE BIOGRAPHY:** In addition to the resume, write a one page biography of your past experience. This does not mean details of early childhood or marital or family problems nor criticism of past employers. Make sure there are no historical gaps. Be specific and be brief.

**THE COVERING LETTER:** Either hand-write or type your covering letter. Some employers prefer a letter in your own handwriting. Those who have made a study of graphology will insist on it. Use plain bond paper. If you feel so inclined have your name printed on a conservatively designed letterhead. Do not use gimmicks or flamboyance in your presentation or you will create suspicion. Don't undersell nor oversell yourself. Present your qualifications truthfully. Your covering letter, your resumé and biography are your entré to the prospective employer's office. Make them interesting. Why should this company hire you over fifty or so other applicants? Think of a good reason and present it in your letter in a concise way.

Management consultants have told me that they receive on an average, about fifty applications for each position advertised and out of the fifty, only eight or so are worthy of calling for an interview. Effective written and oral communication therefore, is a necessary ingredient in selling yourself to others.

**THE INTERVIEW:** Know what the job entails you are applying for. Find out all you can about the company before you apply. Think up reasons why you would be the ideal man for the job. Think of sensible questions to ask the interviewer. Go over in your mind possible questions you will be asked and think of intelligent answers to give.

---

# 4 HELPFUL POINTERS

1. THINK ABOUT THE POSITION YOU SEEK

2. PREPLAN AND ARRIVE WITH QUESTIONS AND ANSWERS

3. DRESS NEATLY, COMFORTABLY AND CONSERVATIVELY

4. CREATE A FAVOURABLE IMAGE

---

When you are introduced to your interviewer, greet him with a warm smile, a strong handshake and maintain eye contact at all times. Don't look at the floor or the ceiling, he'll think you have something to hide or lack confidence. Your education may be impressive but it won't always guarantee you a job. Your personality, dress and manners, plus education and previous experience will.

**SOME DO'S AND DON'TS.** Don't oversell yourself. Make the interviewer aware in a confident way of your qualifications and the reasons you feel you are the man for the job. Don't ask inane questions or give hazy answers. One of the most irksome things you can do is to start enquiring about vacations and benefits. Know exactly what salary you desire. Know what the job will demand of your talents. If possible, come to the interview with a suggested plan of action you would propose to implement should you be employed. Be forthright, do not try and mislead your interviewer. If you were fired from a previous position tell him so and the reason why. If you lie, you will be found out. Never negate a previous employer. Loyalty is valued by *all* employers.

**ATTENTION TO DRESS AND MANNERS.** A good executive image is important and part of that image is created by your manner of dress. Proper dress and manners are of more importance in a job interview than the unwary would suspect. Dress sense is a matter of commonsense and good taste. Avoid sweaters under suit jackets, pens in the breast pocket of jackets. Both men and women should wear clothes of a conservative colour and cut.

**FOR THE MAN :** Highly polish your shoes and make sure they are in a good state of repair. Wear a clean white, coloured or striped business shirt and a conservative tie. You nails and hair should be well groomed. Avoid throwing your hands around, using cliches or bad language in your speech or in any way acting in an offensive manner. Do not sit down until you are asked. Do not smoke, even if you are asked. Have a list of references with addresses and phone numbers, which can be easily checked.

**FOR THE WOMAN :** Women should dress in a current fashion, but never in an extreme way. Mini skirts are fine, but never on a job interview. A neat hairstyle is of utmost importance. Just as important is your make-up. Remember, you are applying for a business position not a television program. Fresh gloves, neat shoes, unwrinkled stockings, conservative, crisp dress and a small handbag are the dress requirements. A reminder: never prop your bag down on the interviewer's desk. It is bad manners as well as being distracting.

Interviews for some people are often quite nerve wracking. The more preparation you do for your interview the less nerve wracking and the more successful it will be.

136

# SUMMARY OF IDEAS TO REAP
# A GOLDEN HARVEST OF
# RICHES

1. *KNOW WHAT YOU WANT—Clearly define what it is you want in this life. God has supplied you with the necessary equipment to succeed but you have to supply the specific goals and the desire to succeed.*

2. *DON'T WANDER THROUGH LIFE WITHOUT A PLAN OF ACTION—Formulate a* **master plan** *and use it as a guidepost to success. Pursue your goals in a scientific way by* **planning** *every step of the way.*

3. *ENLIST THE AID OF OTHERS—Gather an* **action group** *around you, a group of experts who know the things you cannot be expected to know.*

4. *TACKLE ONE GOAL AT A TIME—Don't try to accomplish too much at once. Take things step by step or you will end up in a confused and frustrated state.*

5. *FORMULATE IDEAS—Ideas count; everything begins with an idea. Good ideas are worth fortunes as many creative idea developers have found out. OBSERVE-INQUIRE-QUESTION-THINK.*

# HOW TO OVERCOME PROBLEMS BY MAKING THE RIGHT DECISIONS

*Success Ideas in this Chapter*

**10** *There is nothing in the world more pitiable than an irresolute man, oscillating between two feelings, who would willingly unite the two, and who does not perceive that nothing can unite them.*

GOETHE

**MAKE UP YOUR OWN MIND—THE SECRET OF MAKING DECISIONS.** This book cannot pay your bills, get you the job you desire, restore your health, sell your house, patch up your family differences or cure your frustrations, anxieties or worries. This book can, however, challenge you to harness your conscious and sub-conscious powers so that you are able to do these things for yourself by making the right decisions.

Too many times we ask others to make decisions for us concerning personal problems. Personal problem solving is a do-it-yourself operation. When people give you advice and say 'you should do this' or 'you shouldn't do that', they are usually passing judgement based on secondhand knowledge and seldom on the facts. This amounts to a secondhand opinion which is worth very little.

Don't allow others to sway the decisions you make. Whatever the views expressed by other people keep in mind that they are putting forth 'opinions'. Base your decisions on *facts* and never allow yourself to be swayed from the truth by a secondhand opinion. The opinions of others are never a safe guide. RULE: *fact over opinion always*.

**FOLLOW THE ADVICE OF A SYDNEY ENTREPRENEUR.** A well-known Sydney entrepreneur was asked by a reporter to state his ambition for the next 10 years. 'To cease listening to the advice of other people. All my mistakes have come about because I listened to others.

My gambles pay off more times than not if I follow my own tastes,' was the reply. A wise decision indeed.

**GET THE FACTS BEFORE YOU DRAW CONCLUSIONS.** When important decisions are to be made, surround yourself with pertinent information that will assist in your final judgement. Give yourself time to understand the problem. If other people are able to bring you facts and figures, listen to them, talk against them, weigh the consequences, look for distorted facts, then make your decision and stick by it. Right or wrong, you will have only yourself to blame if the outcome is less than favourable. The important thing is, *you* will have made up your own mind.

It takes courage to solve problems and make important decisions, as every individual who applies at the leadership counter finds out. If you are willing to tackle problems intelligently, draw your own conclusions and make clear-cut decisions, you are showing the mark of a self power.

**HOW PRESIDENT KENNEDY ARRIVED AT A DECISION THAT AVERTED WORLD WAR III.** During the Cuban missile crisis, which began on Tuesday morning, 16 October, 1962, the United States and Russia came perilously close to igniting a third world war. A miscalculation, a misunderstanding, a wrong decision from either Kennedy or Khrushchev could have meant war.

Russia had installed missiles in Cuba—missiles pointed in the direction of major U.S. cities—missiles that could kill millions of Americans in minutes. President Kennedy was faced with a perilous decision: invade Cuba and risk a direct confrontation with Russia or impose a blockade and attempt by peaceable methods to convince Khrushchev to withdraw the offensive weapons. Which was it to be? The world waited.

The President sought the assistance of his top advisers. They talked, argued and debated the ultimate course of action. Recommendations and opinions came from every quarter of Government. Yet, the final decision, one that could change the course of history, was entirely in the hands of one man—John F. Kennedy.

J.F.K. wisely wanted to hear from people who raised questions and challenged and criticized all the possible consequences of any particular course of action. The President knew that many times men will adapt their pattern of thinking to what they believe the other person wants to hear. There could be no room for a decision based on the advice of such individuals in this case, the end result was too important.

Kennedy made his decision based on the best possible information supplied to him by his advisers. For America—and indeed the world—it was a correct decision. The missiles were withdrawn, Russia saved face by not being made to 'eat crow' and a nuclear holocaust was averted. This is decision making at its highest level—cool, calm, confident—and above all, *right*.

**EFFECTIVE DECISION MAKING TAKES COURAGE.** The ability to make *effective* decisions is an absolute necessity for those who want to become leaders. It is one thing to be able to make a decision, but it is another, to act on it. Those who procrastinate or are neutral on whether to make an investment, purchase a car, change their job or take a trip, bring confusion into their lives and rarely achieve happiness and success. These are the people who cannot seem to make up their minds about anything—and they are the *constant losers*.

No one would deny that it takes a great deal of inner strength to make decisions on personal problems, events and situations and then *act* on the decisions that have been made. Decision making cannot be avoided. If you wish to experience a normal existence then you must be prepared to face up to problems and situations, courageously decide on a definite course of action, then stick with it.

**THREE STEPS TO MAKING EFFECTIVE DECISIONS.** The most important ingredients for making affective decisions are:

1. *ARGUE* the pros and cons.

2. *BELIEVE* in your final decision.

3. *HOLD* to your decision and see it through.

## 1. THE ARGUE METHOD

Look at the *facts* concerning your problem. What are they? Write them down. Analyse them. There is always a *right* and a *wrong* side. What are the good points? What are the adverse points? Your decisions must be practical and based on given facts. Do not make up your mind on a course of action until you have carefully considered the issues at hand. *Rationalize*. Don't make decisions based on your emotions, but intelligently, with the mind. If your thoughts are wise, your decisions will be wise.

You shape your destiny by the calibre of your thoughts and the calibre of the decisions you make. Your decisions set your circumstances. You improve your circumstances by improving your thinking and the decisions you make. Good thoughts and good decisions can never produce bad results. *According to your decision is it done unto you.*

## 2. BELIEVE IN YOUR DECISIONS

Once you've made a decision and it is final, believe in it. Don't be wishy-washy or feel you've done the wrong thing. Unless you have faith in your ability to 'decide' and *believe* in the decisions you make, your chances of making the right decisions in the future will be slim.

Even if some of your decisions turn out to be poor ones, don't give up or feel that every decision you make will be a wrong one. The very fact that you've made a decision at all, puts you ahead. With each new decision you make, you are that much more experienced in the art of *effective decision making* and better able to cope with anything of a negative nature that might crop up in the future.

### 3. HOLD TO YOUR DECISIONS

There is little point in making decisions unless you intend to stick to them. You must discipline your mind to abide by your decisions. Get into the habit of deciding on small things. Decide what you will wear tomorrow, what your schedule will be, what you will eat for lunch. Stick to your decisions. Gradually decide on more important issues and as you persist in this affirmative way, all of your decisions— big and small—will be successful ones.

**DON'T RESENT THE OPINIONS OF OTHERS.** Resentment of other people's opinions and decisions is immature thinking. When you blow up because you disagree with a decision made by another and you criticize him for it, you are building up resentment in the other person that will work against you. Resentment breeds resentment. Don't personalise criticism. Don't be over sensitive to the way others think and decide. They feel their point of view is right or they wouldn't have arrived at a decision at all. Give others your confidence, particularly if they are experts, and let them know that you value their opinions. Give them a chance to show their worth.

Don't jump to conclusions before you have the facts. When you do have them, make sure you have them straight before you act on them. Call for the facts. Discuss them quietly. Take each man's point of view and weigh it. Don't complicate that which is clear. Don't waste time and energy arguing over meaningless points.

**LEARN FROM YOUR MISTAKES.** Dwight D. Eisenhower, in an article in *Reader's Digest* 'What is Leadership', recalls an incident during the second world war when he had cause to demote a major general to lieutenant colonel because of mistakes in judgement.

'Many men when confronted with this sort of personal defeat in World War II, were completely crushed. In this case, however, the officer accepted my decision without the slightest bitterness. Not only that, he requested transfer to another combat unit and distinguished himself, rising to brigadier general in combat and again to major general. He had the unusual capacity to admit error and learn from it,' wrote General Eisenhower. RULE: *When you're wrong, admit to it. Don't resent others of authority telling you that you are wrong. Learn from your mistakes.*

**AN OBSTINATE MIND WON'T ABSORB NEW IDEAS.** If you seem to be making mistakes continually it is because you are clinging to false beliefs. You can correct your mistakes by correcting your beliefs. Scrutinize what you 'think' about the things on which you need to make a decision. Are your beliefs really prejudices? Are you obstinate because of childish pride? Do you cling to beliefs of the past because 'what was good enough then, is good enough now'?

An obstinate mind cannot take hold of new ideas. When you hold to fixed beliefs it is difficult to grasp fresh ideas. You do yourself an injustice by limiting your intellectual growth when you limit your inflow of new ideas. Obstinate thinking leads to emotional confusion and poor decision making.

**USE THE L.B.J. METHOD TO PERSUADE OTHERS.** During his term of office, President Lyndon Johnson was admired and respected for his powers of persuasion which many felt were unrivalled. L.B.J. believes that men are moved not by argument but by 'influence'. The former President rarely argued—he *influenced.*

If there is to be an important decision made at a board meeting or a sales conference, don't allow yourself to become involved in heated argument. When men are engaged in heated argument they become adamant and it is difficult to shift them from their points of view.

Heated arguments are a waste of time and lead to faulty thinking and inadequate problem solving because of emotional confusion. You cannot reason intelligently when you are engaged in attacking someone because of his different point of view. You are apt to win your point by 'beating him down' verbally, because you are stronger at oratory than he, but you could lose the final battle. It is senseless to attempt to make a decision or solve a problem by ridiculing the other fellow's point of view. He has as much right to his view as you have to yours. Your job is to 'persuade' him to see your side. If you believe that you are 'right' and your decision is based on fact—not emotional appeal or hear-say—then use the L.B.J. method and *persuade* others to follow your line of thinking.

It's said, 'you can lead a horse to water, but you cannot make him drink'. *Lead* others to your point of view then *persuade* them to adopt it by quietly presenting the facts that have influenced your own decision.

**DON'T BE TRAPPED INTO MAKING DECISIONS WHEN ANGRY.** If in discussion with others, they become angry, remove the negative response before you continue to present your case. Their anger may have been brought about because you wounded their ego. Don't react to their anger by becoming angry yourself. Don't allow others to trap you into becoming angry. Stop them in their tracks and say: 'Let's take a second look at this problem from another point of view. We seem to be confused, not by the situation itself, but by our combined response to it.' Anger stems rational thinking. RULE: *Don't become involved in senseless heated argument—you can't win.*

### ONCE YOU'VE MADE YOUR DECISION DON'T WORRY—FORGET ABOUT IT.

Do all your worrying before you make decisions then once you've made them, forget about them. It makes no sense at all, to leave the gate open, in the hope that the horse won't get out, and when he does, to start fretting and worrying because of your stupidity. The time to worry, if you must worry at all, is when the problem arises. Get your worrying done then. Make a decision on what you are going to do, do it, then forget about it. If you keep worrying about the decision you have made and feel that you have done the wrong thing, you will bring about mental and physical illnesses.

Worry will not solve your problems, change the outcome of them or help you in any way after your decisions have been executed. Make up your mind to stop worrying and fretting and becoming anxious over the decisions you make.

Psychologists still ponder why gamblers joyfully place their bets *then* worry about the outcome. Once you've made your move, it's done; *forget about it.*

### EMOTION DESTROYS RATIONAL THINKING.

The quickest way to make a bad decision is to decide on something when you are emotionally distraught. When you are hostile, anxious, fearful or angry, you cannot think rationally. Your thinking powers are unable to function with any degree of clarity. Learn to postpone all important decision making until you have had ample time to 'calm down' and can see things from another angle. Many times, problem situations are not as bad as they appear to be. Perhaps the wrong facts have been presented or someone has swayed you with a false point of view. Take your time, slow down, see the problem in its true light before you pass judgement on it.

### DON'T ANSWER LETTERS WHEN UPSET.

Never write a letter when you are angry. It could get you into legal trouble. Wait a day or two before answering mail that has made you angry. This gives you and the other party time to cool down and to realize that an equitable solution can be worked out.

### PUT YOUR PROBLEMS IN WRITING.

Decide upon one problem at a time, if several situations of a negative nature confront you. Sort them out, write them down in the order in which you wish to dispose of them. The one requiring immediate attention should be tackled first. Reduce each problem to a single sentence. A problem reduced to a single sentence is less likely to confuse you than the same problem spread over several pages.

After you've stated the problem in one strong sentence, write down the facts, add two possible solutions, consider the consequences of each, then make your decision and immediately act upon it.

When you are involved in making important decisions, never make them while you are ill, emotionally upset or when you have had a little too much to drink or you will add further problems to those you already have.

Decide this very moment to stand up to your problems. Don't let them bring you to your knees; know that faith in the power of your subconscious will open the door and show you how to make important decisions and help you to solve every difficulty that may arise.

**EVERY PROBLEM HAS A SOLUTION.** There is no problem on the face of this earth that does not have a solution. Every problem known to man has been solved a thousand-and-one times by a thousand-and-one others. Even though your problem may seem unique to you, others have experienced it and solved it. Man creates his own problems, therefore, man has the answers to his problems. There is always a way out. Concealed within each problem is a hidden truth. Once this 'truth of the situation' is discovered, the answer is revealed. To all of us is given a choice; we can struggle with the problem or we can search for the hidden truth of the situation that will unlock the door to the perfect solution. Problems are like jig-saw puzzles, once the missing piece is found, the other pieces fall into place.

Too many people get in their own way when attempting to solve problems. They cloud the situation with too many negative aspects. They become obsessed with the outcome and what *might* happen. This continual thinking of the 'trouble' only enlarges it, for the subconscious mind magnifies what is put into it.

Stop thinking of the trouble, whatever it is. As long as you allow your mind to become riveted on the problem, you are going to reproduce more of the same. Centre your attention on the *solution* you want. Let the 'reaction' to the situation go. It is not the problem itself that will bring you to your knees, it is your *reaction* to it. A negative reaction renders your thinking powers inoperable for finding an effective solution. Your object is to expel the thought of any difficulty right out of your consciousness and substitute an affirmative attitude toward finding a suitable solution.

If you indulge in negative thoughts or accept negative suggestions and allow them to affect you emotionally, these ideas will hamper your rational understanding of the problem at hand and seriously affect the final decision you do make.

If a particular problem is worrying you and you are wondering about the answer, try to solve it objectively. Get every scrap of information available. The current information could vastly alter previously formed impressions.

There is no power whatsoever in any problem until you *give power* to the problem to affect you emotionally. Fear of the outcome of any situation is your greatest enemy. True thinking is free from fear. Focus your thoughts on the solution to your problem; ask the right questions to get the right answers. Examine all the alternatives, then *act*, knowing that you have done all you possibly can do under the circumstance.

**YOUR SUBCONSCIOUS MIND HAS THE ANSWER.** If you are confronted with a problem and you cannot see an immediate answer, assume that your subconscious already has the solution and is waiting to reveal it to you. If an answer does not come, turn the problem over to your deeper mind prior to sleep. Keep on turning your request over to your subconscious until the answer comes.

There is no problem too great for the subconscious to solve, for the deeper mind is *One with the Mind of God*. Rama Krishna taught that life's problems could be solved simply if humans realized that 'God is in everything and the answer to all problems lies within the mind of man'.

Mentally devote yourself to the answer you want. The subconscious will always answer you, if you trust it. The response will be a certain 'feeling', an inner awareness, whereby you 'know' what to do. Guidance in all things comes as the *still small voice within*; it reveals all. The answer you seek could come while you are driving, while you are in your office or home or when you are about to go off to sleep. An 'inner awareness' of what is *right* is suddenly there.

**GIVE YOURSELF ROOM TO THINK.** Sit quietly at your desk or in a comfortable chair in your home and give yourself a few silent moments to think freely. True thinking is *relaxed* thinking. Contemplate right action taking place as you seek guidance in overcoming all that bothers you. As you focus your mind on the solution to your problem, believe that you have the answer now. Feel the happiness associated with the right answer. Your subconscious will respond to your feeling and whether at that moment or later, will bring the answer to you.

Make the following affirmation: *The power of my subconscious mind knows and reveals to me all that I need to know. A perfect solution is mine now.*

**THE CANADIAN TECHNIQUE TO SOLVE PROBLEMS.** Many executives I know quietly use the abstract term 'solution' when a problem arises and they repeat it until the solution comes. This is turning the problem over to the subconscious, which always has the answer.

A Canadian politician friend uses this method to find the solutions to the many problems that confront him as a senior Government official in Ottawa. He repeats throughout the day: 'there is a solution to this problem and the perfect answer is being revealed by my subconscious mind.'

**PICTURE THE OUTCOME OF EVERY PROBLEM ON YOUR MENTAL SCREEN.** If you are presented with a situation that requires a major decision, one that involves marriage or business or affects the lives of others, retire to a quiet place where you can direct your entire attention to the problem at hand. It might be a park, a room away from others in your home or office, perhaps even a visit to a church. Find a tranquil setting where you can relax, let go of worldly things, still your mind and think out your problem.

Place yourself into a meditative state, close your eyes and fill your mental screen with a picture of how you want your problem to be resolved. Throw out false mental pictures of the past. Negative mental pictures impressed into the subconscious become 'desires to be completed' by the deeper mind.

Whenever problems require solving, turn to your mental screen and picture the outcome. *Know* that your affirmative mental image will repeat itself in your outer world. To do so, is to live in the expectancy of the affirmative.

**FEAR DESTROYS YOUR ABILITY TO MAKE EFFECTIVE DECISIONS.** Fear comes from indecision about a problem. Fear is man's greatest enemy. It is the major cause of failure. Fear breeds on negative thoughts and ideas and paralyses mental powers. Fear is a phantom; it isn't something we can touch, yet it can destroy us. People literally worry themselves to death because of their *fear* of things.

Your subconscious mind accepts your 'fears' as a desire to concede defeat. Whatever you 'imagine' to be true, will be developed by your subconscious mind and will come to pass. The subconscious always accepts the stronger of two ideas. Abnormal fear comes about by allowing your imagination to 'run wild' in a negative way. The subconscious accepts negative suggestions and sets them into motion.

Fear also comes about because of ignorance of the true facts about any given situation. Don't waste mental energy fearing something you know nothing about. Don't jump to conclusions. Don't guess. Find out the facts before you draw your conclusions; a conclusion without the facts is false. Reject theories if they are not in line with facts. When fear creeps in, examine it; hold it up to the light and see through it, dissolve it by knowing the truth about the problem.

An affirmative mental attitude allows no room for fear. A healthy attitude of mind dissolves fear as it crops up. Fear has no power of its own, only the power 'built up' and given it by those who are habitual negative thinkers. Change negative thoughts and you'll destroy fear.

If you are in an unpleasant situation, refrain from fearing it. Know that your subconscious mind already knows the way out and is revealing it to you.

**NEVER COMPROMISE YOUR IDEALS.** Never permit others to take advantage of you and win their point by anger, hostile methods or any form of mental blackmail. Some people will attempt to win by any means they can think up and will try to put 'one over' you if you are foolish enough to let them get away with it. Appeasement is not the answer. Once you back down on your decisions or bow to pressure, others soon lose respect for you, even though you may have bowed to their wishes. Those who use mental blackmail are little more than bullies, attempting to force you to think the way they think.

Allow no one to dictate the way you should think. You have the right of freedom of thought—exercise it. Let no one turn you from your aims in life, the decisions you make or the manner in which you wish to express your talents. *Stand firm.* Always do that which is 'right' regardless of what others may think or feel. Honesty pays.

Permit others to differ with you. They have a right to oppose your view point just as you have the freedom to disagree with theirs, but don't allow them to walk over you. This is a sure sign of a weakling. When you refuse to be trampled on, bullied into making decisions or mentally blackmailed into doing things you are opposed to, you will quickly command the respect of others. *Your personal integrity should be worth more to you than anything else*; remain *true* to yourself. Honesty of speech and actions pays remarkable dividends.

# SUMMARY OF IDEAS ON HOW
# TO MAKE EFFECTIVE DECISIONS

1. *Don't ask others to make decisions for you. Effective decision making is a do-it-yourself project.*

2. *Surround yourself with the facts. Look for distorted facts, weed them out.*

3. *Argue the pros and cons. Know what you are getting into. See the consequences of your final decision. Once you've made your decision and acted on it, forget about it. Don't worry about the outcome.*

4. *Don't let people become hostile when discussing problems that require an important decision. Clear thinking is the answer, not heated arguments and temper tantrums.*

5. *Use the* **L.B.J.** *method.* **Persuade** *others to see your point of view, don't try to brow beat them into accepting it. You might win the point but lose the battle.*

6. *Never make important decisions when you are angry, ill or in any way emotionally disturbed. Never answer a letter while you are in this frame of mind.*

7. *Put your problems in writing.*

8. *Turn your problem over to your subconscious mind. Repeat 'solution' throughout your day. Know that your subconscious has the answer and will reveal it to you.*

9. *Visualize the outcome of your problem. Picture it in your mind's eye as you want it to be.*

10. *Never compromise your ideals or allow others to mentally blackmail you into making decisions you know are wrong. Stand up for your right of free thought.*

# HOW TO ACQUIRE THE
# IMAGE OF A STAR

## *Success Ideas in this Chapter*

- You Become What You THINK You Are
- You May Not Know It But You Are Tops
- The Two Types Of Image
- The SELF Image
- Unlock The REAL You
- How To Gain An Effective SELF Image
- The Projected Image
- How To Gain An Effective PROJECTED Image
- Before You Change Your Old Image Paint A Mental Canvas Of The New One
- That Elusive STAR Quality. What Is It And How Can You Attain It?
- Be Charming And You'll Be Liked
- A Smile Is The Best Calling Card
- Everything You Say And Do Counts On The First Introduction
- Don't Try To Win Everyone Or You'll Win No One
- If You Want To Look Like A Star Dress Like A Star
- Simplicity Is The Essence Of Good Taste
- Learn The Art Of Public Speaking
- What You Say And How You Say It Tells All
- 20 Do's And Don'ts Of Public Speaking
- Learn From Other Speakers
- You Are Judged By Your Associates
- Family Relationships Can Build Or Destroy
- Know Your Real Worth
- Don't Belittle Others
- Annoying Habits Detract From Your Personality
- 10 Annoying Habits To Watch
- Don't Put Yourself In Solitary Confinement
- Advance Confidently And Conquer
- Don't Crawl Out Of Bed. CHARGE OUT!
- Strive For Maturity. It's A Sign Of Greatness
- You Are Worthy Of The Best—THINK It—CLAIM It
- Constructing Your Own Image Profile
- Summary Of Ideas To Help You Develop An Effective Image

# 11

*The common phrase, 'building a personality' is a misnomer.—Personality is not so much like a structure as like a river—it continuously flows, and to be a person is to be engaged in a perpetual process of becoming.*

HARRY EMERSON FOSDICK

---

YOU BECOME WHAT YOU THINK YOU ARE. An effective and self-satisfying concept of 'self' is the key to balanced human behaviour. An affirmative self concept or *self image* opens the door to creative accomplishment. When you establish an adequate image of yourself, you start becoming what you 'think' you are. If you wish to be a leader of men, possess a dynamic personality, be able to make positive decisions, charm others with an eloquent manner, succeed at everything you undertake, then create a mental picture of yourself filling all of these roles. You create a new image of yourself by building into it all the qualities you desire. Your image is your calling card, a sign around your neck stating to all: 'this is who I am'.

YOU MAY NOT KNOW IT BUT YOU ARE TOPS! You are a creative human being—the highest creation on this planet in fact. You are great; you are clever; you are brilliant; you are attractive; you are an intelligent being capable of high accomplishment; but you are a fool if you do not know it and take advantage of it.

You may not have considered yourself to be all of these things, but nevertheless, that is how you are. Unfortunately, most people fail to acknowledge their greatness. They under-rate and under-sell themselves. They project an inadequate self image that others see, judge, accept and react to. Who should you blame when others size you up as being 'a little dull'? Certainly not your detractors, for they have

155

judged you on the ineffectual image you yourself have put forth. An English proverb suggests: *You may find the worst enemy or best friend in yourself.*

The image we hold of others is not only a picture in our minds eye of them physically, but also a judgement of their worth. When another person meets you for the first time, he forms a definite opinion. He judges you on your appearance and manner and on the way you speak and react. This *image* that forms in his mind is the image *you* have created and the one you are carrying around for *all* to see—good or bad.

**THE TWO TYPES OF IMAGE.** It is necessary to formulate two aspects of an effective image. The first is the *self image*: 'the person I think I am'. The second is the *projected image*: 'the type of person I want others to immediately see and respect'.

**THE SELF IMAGE.** Your self image is the sort of person 'I think I am'. It is the mental, physical and spiritual picture you hold of yourself. It is your private and deep down opinion of what *you* think you are. It is an evaluation of what you *are*, what you *have* and what you think you *can* be. Once a mental blueprint has been formulated by your conscious mind, it is accepted by your subconscious as 'the way I am'. What you *think* you are, you then become. Imagine yourself to be a failure type and that's the way you will end up.

An adequate self image is one of the greatest assets you can have. It equips you with that indefinable 'something' that other men admire.

Your self image works effectively for you when you believe that you are a worthwhile, creative and intelligent human being. When you cultivate an effective self image you join the ranks of the successful. *Image and perceive that which you want to be and you will be.*

**UNLOCK THE REAL YOU.** Pour enthusiasm and love into your self image. What you seek begins with what you have; you then build from there. Gain a solid belief in what you *are* and project this belief confidently in what you say and what you do. Think of the way you want to be, the things you know you can do and the 'self' you wish others to know and accept. In other words, *think* your new image, *feel* your new image and *act* your new image.

To gain an effective self image does not mean that you have to drastically change your basic self. But you do have to change the basic estimation you hold in your mind of yourself. When you enhance your estimation of yourself, your abilities, behaviour, feelings and actions improve. You unlock the *real* you. Your personality is released and you are able to express your true self.

## HOW TO GAIN AN EFFECTIVE *SELF* IMAGE

I NEED TO CHANGE MY NEGATIVE ATTITUDES TOWARD LIFE

I NEED TO CHANGE MY SELF CONDEMNATION

I NEED TO CHANGE MY LACK OF CONFIDENCE IN MY ABILITIES

I NEED TO CHANGE MY TIMID MANNER

I NEED TO CHANGE MY FEAR OF FAILURE

I NEED TO CHANGE MY DESTRUCTIVE THOUGHTS

I NEED TO CHANGE MY LAZINESS PATTERN


**THE PROJECTED IMAGE.** Your projected image is the personality and appearance others see and judge you on. It is a combination of your inner and outer qualities. In addition to the way you think and speak, it includes: facial expression, smile, eye contact, posture, walk, dress.

A package can look interesting or dull depending upon how well it has been 'dressed up'. Poor packaging of products results in poor sales. Exciting and colourful packaging returns high sales. Any good advertising man would confirm this.

## HOW TO GAIN AN EFFECTIVE *PROJECTED* IMAGE

I NEED TO CHANGE MY BAD MANNERS

I NEED TO CHANGE MY DULL PERSONALITY

I NEED TO CHANGE MY POOR PHYSICAL APPEARANCE

I NEED TO CHANGE MY SLOPPY DRESS

I NEED TO CHANGE MY INARTICULATE SPEECH PATTERN

I NEED TO CHANGE MY TOO-ANIMATED FACIAL EXPRESSIONS

I NEED TO CHANGE MY EXAGGERATED GESTURES


**BEFORE YOU CHANGE YOUR OLD IMAGE PAINT A MENTAL CANVAS OF THE NEW ONE.** Before you change your personality you must see yourself in a new personality role. Picture yourself as you want to be. Paint a canvas in your mind of how you wish to look. Your mental picture 'believed in', is the strongest force within you.

Personality, charm, confidence, wit, are qualities that take time and effort to develop. Commence painting your mental canvas right now. Little by little, day by day, your picture of 'self' will take shape as you create, plan and develop it. Get to know your strengths and weaknesses and what you actually want out of life. As your new self image takes shape your life will begin to expand. You will cease to be 'wrapped up' in yourself. You will become aware of 'others' and 'things' in a new light.

THAT ELUSIVE STAR QUALITY—WHAT IS IT AND HOW CAN YOU ATTAIN IT? What is the magic quality that famous television and film stars have that distinguishes them from the average individual? To most people it's quite difficult to define. I've posed this question to the stars themselves and even they are vague in their attempts to pinpoint 'what makes a star'. Certainly no one would deny that Clark Gable, Gary Cooper, Humphrey Bogart, Tyrone Power, Errol Flynn, all possessed a certain 'something' that endeared them to millions of theatre goers around the world. This same magic personality ingredient has kept stars such as: Joan Crawford, Lucille Ball, Barbara Stanwyck, and Marlene Dietrich in front of the public eye for 25 years or more. The best description of 'star quality' I have heard was given during a television interview I conducted with George Pal, the M.G.M. producer of 'The Wonderful World of the Brothers Grimm'. Mr Pal summed it up in one word—PROJECTION.

Cary Grant may be tall and handsome but he *projects* inner qualities of warmth, charm, interest, and an infectious vibrancy that jumps from the screen and keeps women swooning the world over.

*Stars project.* Stars jump out from the silver screen and literally touch you. They project a definite image that has *appeal.* They may be acting out situations as characters other than themselves, but their personal magnetism always shines through. And so can yours, if you allow it to shine. Open up your mind and heart and pour forth love, wisdom, charm, humility and an exuberance that spells out a magnificent YOU that others admire and respect.

BE CHARMING AND YOU'LL BE LIKED. Charm depends on a genuine interest *in* and enjoyment *of* other people. When you make others aware of their own identity and worth, they will find you charming.

Charm is graciousness of manner, warmth, a sense of humour, lack of egotism and a genuine caring about those you are with. If you want to be liked, learn to be charming.

A SMILE IS THE BEST CALLING CARD. A sincere, warm smile will disarm even the most unpleasant of individuals. One of the fundamental laws of life is that of reciprocity. Because it is a simple law it is one that is often ignored. This law, when practised, has a chain reaction effect. Snarl at a man when you are first introduced and he will react to you in like manner. Humans respond to one another emotionally instead of 'thinkingly', thus, petty jealousies, hate, bruised egos, fights and wars.

It is important *how* you greet others. Their first impression of you is based on your words, deeds and general appearance. Always greet people in a friendly way, regardless of their attitude toward you. *Life is action and reaction.* Take the initiative, smile, be pleasant. You will soon find that others will *react* to your friendly approach and smile back.

There is a simple story that highlights the above philosophy. A teacher wished to express the action-reaction idea to his class. He handed a young boy and girl five pennies each and told them to go separate ways and to throw away a penny each time they met someone who smiled.

Eventually, the youngsters returned. The young boy still had in his possession all five pennies. The young girl had given away hers. The boy complained that the people he met did not smile. 'But all mine did', cut in the girl, 'because I smiled first.' Therein lies the secret; if you want the world to smile at you, take the initiative and smile first.

Movie stars win fans by their sincere, warm and friendly smiles. A smile breaks down another's coldness. *Smile*—and often.

**EVERYTHING YOU SAY AND DO COUNTS ON THE FIRST INTRODUCTION.** 'You always meet people a second time', is the advice given by Samuel Goldwyn, the Hollywood producer. Meaning of course, that the way you treat others the first time you meet them is important, because even though it may be years later, you are apt to meet them again and they will remember how you treated them.

*Good first impressions* are important. Never forget that. The things you say and the way you act the very first time you meet someone, largely determines the reception you will receive from them the next time. If you are unpleasant and rude, that's how you will be remembered.

Do not act as though you do not care whether you ever meet again the person you are being introduced to. The person on the bottom rung of the ladder today could well be the individual who has the power to employ your services or buy your product tomorrow. It may be years later, but the image you present today could come back to haunt you at some future time.

Individual impressions stay with people: 'He was that smart aleck.' 'That's the dishonest one.' 'I remember she was the person who was rude and insulting to me,' are statements I've heard made about others who were being considered for employment by company executives. Watch what you say and do when you are being introduced, always be pleasant.

**DON'T TRY TO WIN EVERYONE OR YOU'LL WIN NO ONE.** Be yourself when you are being introduced to others. Don't try to impress people with smart remarks or an overbearing personality. Others will resent you for it. Be natural. Don't try to win everyone or you'll wind up winning no-one. The only person you should be concerned about pleasing is *yourself*. Be yourself. Certainly take advantage of your personality to express it effectively, but never in any way likely to óffend others or have them remark, 'what an obnoxious individual'.

IF YOU WANT TO LOOK LIKE A STAR, DRESS LIKE A STAR. As part of your projected image it is necessary for you to acquire a flair for dressing well. What you wear and *how* you wear it, is important. The statement, 'clothes make the man', has a lot of truth in it. Top performers pay careful attention to the way they dress. Good looking clothes are a necessary asset to the image of every entertainer.

You are well worth the investment of good clothes. When you are properly dressed you *feel* right and become confident. Good clothes give you a boost, they also give you pride in how you look.

Dressing with elegance is not always a question of money; it is, however, a question of good judgement and taste. Quality, style, expert tailoring in a garment, is the most economical in the long run. Cheap, inferior, poorly made, ill-fitting clothes stick out like a sore thumb. While it is true, some people are born with a unique flair for fashion, others can most surely acquire it. Fashion is knowing what one's own style is and sticking with it. Your wardrobe should express your personality and mode of living and not conform to someone else's taste.

Fashion is a certain feeling for looking your best at all times. It requires some knowledge of cloth, style and fit, but most of all, it requires some good old-fashioned horse sense. You can develop a knowledge of clothes by talking with those who work with them: tailors, salesmen, fashion models, fashion writers, and those who exhibit a clothes sense. Read fashion articles and window shop. The important points to remember when buying clothes are: your *colouring*, your *shape*, your *tastes*, your *budget*.

SIMPLICITY IS THE ESSENCE OF GOOD TASTE. Cary Grant has often won 'Best Dressed' awards. He told me during a press conference that he considers 'simplicity' the best course when selecting clothes. 'Simplicity is the essence of good taste,' he feels.

When you are shopping for clothes make certain that the accessories harmonize with items you already possess. Avoid flashy colours, exaggerated fad styles that are 'in' this season and 'out' the next. High style does not mean outlandish style. It means being one step ahead with elegant garments that do not 'date' quickly.

If budget restricts you, buy fewer clothes but all of them of excellent quality. I would rather have two pairs of quality shoes than four pairs of cheap ones. *Simplicity is the essence of good taste.* Use it as your guide the next time you shop for clothes.

LEARN THE ART OF PUBLIC SPEAKING. If you have never faced an audience from behind the speaker's rostrum, stood before a sales meeting to read a report or had to make a speech at a social function, then it is about time you got your feet wet. Once you've learned the art of public speaking—no matter how timid you may be now—wild horses won't hold you back from jumping to your feet whenever the occasion demands it.

**WHAT YOU SAY AND HOW YOU SAY IT TELLS ALL.** The way you speak is indicative of the level of your intelligence—not your potential level—but the level you are now at and restricting yourself to. What you say is a confession of your weaknesses, triumphs, desires and ambitions. Your language is the expression of your mind. It reveals the inner man. Your voice speaks volumes about you. It tells of your education, your attitudes and your habits. It is wise to spend time and effort improving your language and the way you present it.

Within the limits of this chapter it is not possible to tell all there is to know about public speaking. But there are books available that deal specifically with this subject. Enquire at your library or book store. There are also various speaking groups that meet regularly for the purpose of encouraging people to get up on their feet. (Rostrum and the International Toastmaster and Toastmistress Clubs are listed in your telephone directory).

## 20 DO'S AND DON'TS OF PUBLIC SPEAKING

1. Type your notes on small cards. Use key phrases that lead you into the main points of your text. Do not use large sheets of paper. They are too distracting and look as though you are going to read your speech word for word.

2. Don't read your speech verbatim. Know your subject well. Don't memorize it and spout it off parrot fashion.

3. Unless you are an experienced speaker do not speak 'off the cuff' for an official function. Prepare your subject before hand and *know* what you are going to say. This prevents you saying anything of an embarrassing nature.

4. Watch your voice. Is it too high pitched? Monotonous? Do you mumble? Speak up so that your entire audience can hear every word.

5. Do not eat a hearty meal before you are to speak or it will dull your energy.

6. When you get up to speak, take a deep breath and let it out slowly to dissolve the 'butterflies'.

7. Don't be in a great hurry to start. Settle yourself before you begin. Look at your audience. If there is a noise, wait. Be glad to see them. Smile if you wish. Show interest in them. Your personality contributes to the success of your speech.

8. When you speak, be *enthusiastic* about what you are saying. If you don't care, neither will your audience. 'This subject is important, it means something to us,' should be your attitude.

9. Don't get flustered. Don't be cold. Don't be timid. Don't be boastful.

10. Fan your audience. Take in the back row, the sides and front. Don't drop your head down and thereby cut your effectiveness off from the second row.

11. Gain eye contact from time to time with individuals in the audience. Focus your attention on an individual then move on to someone else. Get *contact* with those you are speaking to.

12. Be careful as to the gestures you use. They must not be mechanical or distracting. Use them to emphasise a point. Gesture from the shoulder to the elbow with ease, not in a jerky manner.

13. If you are using a microphone, stand back from it twelve to eighteen inches so it doesn't 'pop'. Don't shout into a microphone. If your voice has volume step back a pace or two.

14. Know the length of time you have been given to speak and stay strictly within your time limit. You may not be asked to speak a second time if you don't.

15. If you have a dry throat use a pinch of *salt* or *lemon*. Both are better than water.

16. Don't fiddle with your clothes, take your glasses on or off, slouch, grab the rostrum as though you need it to hold you up.

17. Stand still unless you know *how* to move and how to control and use movement for impact.

18. If you have an amusing story that can be used to point up what you are saying, use it.

19. Your voice should *rise and fall*. Don't pound your audience for long stretches. Give them time to 'breathe'. Build to the climax of each point, give your audience a rest then rise again. Watch your pace. Give people time to absorb what you are saying.

20. When you close *restate* your whole speech in one sentence and add a 'something to think about' message to it.

**LEARN FROM OTHER SPEAKERS.** During the dozen or so years I have been a professional motivational speaker in Canada and the U.S., I have met, talked with and watched others in the same profession. I enjoy listening and watching a good platform speaker. I go to *learn* something and always do. Perhaps the main body of a speaker's material I have heard or read before, but I have yet to attend a lecture where I have not come away with ONE point that I have profitably been able to use.

When you attend a lecture, take notes, listen for the main points, get at least *one* idea that is appealing and both you and the speaker will have benefited. You can learn a lot from other speakers. Watch them; listen to them. Watch for their negative and affirmative points, then gradually formulate a speaking style of your own.

Billy Graham is probably one of the most effective platform speakers I have ever heard. Dr Graham knows his subject, knows how to deliver it and how to make his audience sit up, take notice and accept it— surely the mark of any great speaker.

**YOU ARE JUDGED BY YOUR ASSOCIATES.** It is well to remember that others often judge us by the people we associate with. *To see a person's qualities, look closely at his admirers.* An association with the wrong type of individual could affect your progress adversely, should those you wish to influence note this 'wrong association'.

Seek associations with individuals who have a success consciousness. This gives you an opportunity to absorb their knowledge and to harmonize your consciousness with theirs for a greater understanding of life.

Friends with an affirmative consciousness pattern can be likened to good books; they are reliable in their information and they are informative and educational in the knowledge they are able to impart. This is not to suggest that you 'use' friends as a means of reaching goals. You must *give* or your friends won't stay friends very long. This is a world of 'give and take'. Unfortunately, not everyone sees it as such. However, for those desiring lasting success, it is a law to be adhered to.

Size up your present friends and acquaintances and if changes are necessary, ease out of undesirable associations and into new associations with those you can proudly claim are truly your friends, admirers and supporters.

**FAMILY RELATIONSHIPS CAN BUILD OR DESTROY.** Your family relationship says quite a bit about you as a person. Any family that spends more time than it should squabbling, sets a negative personality pattern for each member that can have unfortunate repercussions. For example, a husband who fights continually with his wife reflects this in his dealings with others. He becomes short tempered, intolerant and belligerent and is apt to make poor decisions.

His inner resentment of 'conditions at home' causes his personality to sour. This inadequate image reflects in loss of business, loss of friends and further family discord.

Many married couples fight over the question of authority. Attempting to beat one another into submission over who is going to be boss is childish and frankly futile. Marriage is not a fifty-fifty partnership. It is a 100-per cent partnership whereby each gives *all* to the other by thinking in terms of 'what can I do to make the other person happy and this is a successful marriage?'

Mature individuals are unselfish individuals. They make the best marriage partners because they possess personality traits that make them well adjusted and able to cope with every situation.

**KNOW YOUR REAL WORTH.** Comparing yourself with others is dangerous; it brings fear and inferiority into your life. When you analyse yourself and your abilities in the sight of others and their abilities, you judge yourself unfairly and on a false basis. You are an individual with individual creative talents that others can only imitate. Be convinced of this and know that you are unique.

The genetic variations of man are infinite. There are close to four billion of us populating the earth and except for identical twins, no two of us are alike. Why then, should you waste time and energy comparing yourself with others?

**DON'T BELITTLE OTHERS.** One of the most uncomfortable evenings I have spent was at a dinner party where the host insisted on belittling his wife every time she attempted to join the conversation. She may not have been the most enlightened individual concerning politics—the subject being discussed—but she did put forward several suggestions that I felt added to the conversation. 'That's something she read in a magazine. My wife hasn't a brain in her head,' the husband kept saying.

Some men take great delight in ridiculing and chopping down their wives, subordinates or friends. It may make them feel big, but not in the eyes of others. It is a positive way of showing a petty and bullying character. Squashing the freedom of expression of others is selfish, immature and sinful and should be avoided by those desirious of developing an effective image.

Allow your wife to express her point of view. Compliment her in front of others. Guide her into conversations and encourage her to put forth her views. Every wife is entitled to being shown open appreciation by her husband. Make your wife feel she is your pride and joy—particularly in front of others. A marriage is a happy one when couples build one another *up* instead of tearing one another down.

**ANNOYING HABITS DETRACT FROM YOUR PERSONALITY.**
One of the quickest ways to lose friends and influence people the *wrong* way is to display annoying habits. Ninety-eight per cent of your success in dealing with people is due to your personality. If others can't stand a bar of you, then you aren't going to be too successful in your dealings with them. You've got to make favourable impressions. It takes wit, charm and a vibrant personality to win others to your side. Aggravating speech habits, lack of good manners, sloppy dress and annoying mannerisms are your worst enemies—*get rid of them.*

## 10 ANNOYING HABITS TO WATCH—TICK THE ONES THAT APPLY TO YOU

1. ☐ Stock phrases in your speech.
2. ☐ Mumbling (poor enunciation and articulation).
3. ☐ Careless manners.
4. ☐ Touching people when you talk to them.
5. ☐ Fidgeting, rattling coins when you talk.
6. ☐ Refusing eye contact when talking to people.
7. ☐ Arguing and contradicting for the sake of it.
8. ☐ Scratching, biting nails.
9. ☐ Cutting others off so you can be heard.
10. ☐ Limp handshake.

**DON'T PUT YOURSELF IN SOLITARY CONFINEMENT.** 'Man puts himself in solitary confinement, and he locks the door from the inside. He denies himself the riches of other men's experience. He starves his own mind and he hardens his own heart,' is the well stated opinion of Roy Pearson, Dean of Andover Newton Theological Seminary in Massachusetts. Too much of life is spent keeping people out of it. Man builds fences and posts 'keep out' signs. We see additional evidence of this isolationist attitude in private clubs, private parks and private beaches.

Many people shut out others because they feel insecure in their presence. A strong, confident man is never afraid of others who are 'different' or of those who display greater talents. The mature man welcomes others who show outstanding abilities—he learns from them.

Release yourself from the prison of your mind. Take down the 'no trespassing' sign, draw a huge imaginary circle around you and invite others in. You expand your own personality by mixing with others and learning from them.

# STRIVE FOR MATURITY—
# IT'S A SIGN OF GREATNESS

Maturity comes through knowing the *real you*. It is best summed up in the following eight examples:

1. *Maturity* is patience. It means being able to pass up the fun-for-the-minute things and select the course which will pay off later. One of the characteristics of immaturity is the 'I want it NOW' attitude. Mature people are *patient* people.

2. *Maturity* is the ability to stick with a project until it is completed. The individual who is constantly changing jobs, friends and marriage partners, is immature.

3. *Maturity* is the capacity to face unpleasantness, frustration and defeat without complaint. A mature person knows he can't have everything his own way.

4. *Maturity* is loyalty. Loyalty to your husband or wife, employer, friends.

5. *Maturity* is the ability to live up to your responsibilities. It means *keeping* your word.

6. *Maturity* is integrity.

7. *Maturity* is the ability to make decisions. Immature people explore possibilities then do nothing. Action requires courage.

8. *Maturity* is the ability to harness your creative abilities and to do something worthwhile with them.

**ADVANCE CONFIDENTLY AND CONQUER.** When you have set your goals, adjusted your personality and summoned confidence, advance bravely and do not look back or think of turning back until you have conquered all you have set out to do. Each time you look over your shoulder you sow seeds of distrust in your ability to win. A leader advances; a defeatist retreats.

When Julius Caesar sailed the channel to England with his mighty legions he had them look down from the Cliffs of Dover. They were aghast to see their ships being burnt under Caesar's order. 'You cannot turn back. You have just one choice and that is to advance and conquer,' the mighty leader told them.

Bravely move into the mainstream of life. Draw yourself up to your full height and win by sheer boldness. Do as did Caesar's army— *advance and conquer.*

**DON'T CRAWL OUT OF BED. CHARGE OUT!** Start each day with vim and vigour. When the alarm rings, don't turn it off, roll over and go back to sleep. Don't crawl out of bed feeling as though a steam roller has worked you over during the night, *CHARGE OUT!* Jump up and yell at the top of your lungs— *CHARGE!* Apart from scaring your family witless, the exercise will serve to set you 'on fire' to meet the challenges of the day.

**YOU ARE WORTHY OF THE BEST. THINK IT—CLAIM IT.** You are the sum total of your thoughts. What you think, you become. To *be* something you must think you *are* something. A successful man *thinks* success. He has a high opinion—not conceit—of his own abilities and he sells himself confidently knowing that his confidence rests on the bedrock of previous careful preparation.

Success favours those who expect good things to happen to them. Failure favours those who expect the worst. *Think* and *feel* that you are worthy of the best; always expect the best. Get an attitude, a feeling, a philosophy which gives you 'adequate faith in yourself'. It will be your greatest asset, for your mental states are carried forward into manifestation and become 'experience' through the law of cause and effect.

Your potential is unlimited. Aspire to a high place. Believe in your abilities, in your tastes, in your own judgement. Image and perceive that which you wish to be. Back your image with enthusiasm and courage. Feel the reality of your 'new' self; live in the expectancy of greater things and your subconscious mind will actualize them.

# SUMMARY OF IDEAS TO HELP YOU DEVELOP AN EFFECTIVE IMAGE

1. *Show a genuine interest in others. An 'I couldn't care less' attitude repels people. You* **need** *people to project charm.*

2. *Be enthusiastic at all times. People love to be around an enthusiastic person.* **Look** *alive,* **be** *alive to life and people will swarm around you.*

3. *Move with confidence and a sense of purpose. Don't slouch, look awkward or give a 'sad sack' impression. Eliminate unnecessary gestures. To attract top level people* **act** *like one. Look as though you have a purpose in life and you know where you are going. Speak, walk and act with confidence.*

4. *Listen to yourself when you speak. Is your voice too high pitched? Do you mumble? Is your grammar correct? Do you slur words? Cultivate a well modulated voice that is not affected. Alter the pitch and make yourself sound more mature by speaking in a lower register.*

5. *Dress immaculately, not outlandishly. Hair and fingernails should always be neat and clean.*

6. *Be poised. Have control over your emotions.* **Relax.** *Take everything in stride. Know what you are saying and doing. What you say and do must be* **right,** *logical and* **coherent.**

7. *An effective self image demands that you be a cultured person. Take the time to become acquainted with proper etiquette, music, theatre, art, literature, etc.*

8. *Project a natural personality: be warm, friendly, compassionate, enthusiastic, charming etc. Personality also includes: integrity, wisdom, love, kindess. It excludes: insincerity, false modesty, undue flattery and dishonesty.*

# HOW TO ATTAIN
# MENTAL WELL BEING

## Success Ideas in this Chapter

- How To Avoid Psychosomatic Ills
- To Cure Ills ATTACK The Cause
- If You Are Ill Use The Opposite Technique
- How To Stay Out of Hospital Beds
- Emotional And Physical Ills Brought About By Worry
- Conquer Worry And Escape From The Prison Of Your Mind
- How To Avoid The Blues
- Startling Facts About Suicide
- Set Up A Buffer Against Crisis
- Control Anger And Stem Emotional Illness
- Marital Squabbles Bring Illnesses
- Capture Inner SERENITY With The 5-Minute Vacation Technique
- Be Happy And You'll Be Healthy
- Laughter Is The World's Greatest Medicine
- Copy Rudyard Kipling's Sense of Humour
- Vitamin Pills (And Humour) The Secret of 94-Year-Old's Health
- Spiritual Healing
- The Spiritual Healings Of Phineas Parkhurst Quimby
- Mary Baker Eddy—A Quimby Patient
- Establish FAITH In Your Recovery
- Summary Of Ideas To Help You Attain Mental Well Being

# 12

*If the mind, that rules the body, ever so far forgets itself as to trample on its slave, the slave is never generous enough to forgive the injury, but will rise and smite the oppressor.*

LONGFELLOW

**HOW TO AVOID PSYCHOSOMATIC ILLS.** Specialized research has been going on for many years to discover what effects the mind has over the body. It is now a scientific fact that psychosomatic illnesses are brought about by destructive thoughts, feelings and beliefs. The mental outlook of man can make him healthy or ill, depending on *how* he thinks. Worry, fear, unhappiness, loneliness, tenseness, fatigue caused by overwork, set the scene for physical illnesses by lowering the bodily defences, thus opening the door to germs and infection.

Asthma, migraine, eczema, ulcers, spastic colon, heart disease, are only a few of a host of ailments that have their origins in the mind. Pneumonia is caused when a germ, normally resident in the chest, begins to multiply. Many doctors feel that the reason the germ multiplies is because unhappiness, worry and fatigue have lowered the bodily defences. Fear, hatred, self-pity, envy, jealousy, loneliness, resentment and other negative attitudes are clearly mental poisons that pollute and destroy the body. It is a foolish man indeed who allows his mind to harbour such debilitating attitudes.

**TO CURE ILLS ATTACK THE CAUSE.** In medical terms to 'diagnose' is to recognize the presence of disease from its symptoms. If you are ill the best person to diagnose and help you cure the problem is a qualified doctor. This book does not suggest that you set yourself up as an amateur diagnostician or prescriber of medicines. It does suggest, however, that your learn the rudimentary law of mind: *as a man thinketh in his heart so is he.*

When you practise the principle of affirmative thinking you are attacking the cause of psychosomatic ills and setting up a general immunity to them. It is important to erase from the conscious mind all negative thoughts, ideas and beliefs. *Thoughts are things.* A firm mind producing healthy thoughts produces a healthy body. It is normal and natural to be healthy. It is abnormal to be sick. God did not give you 'life' to have you experience it in sickness and misery. When you conform to the principles of life and change your *thought imagery*, you will change the state of your health.

IF YOU ARE ILL USE THE OPPOSITE TECHNIQUE. If you are sick and wish to be healthy and happy it is necessary to do an 'about face' and think of what you *want* and not what you *are*. To do this is to apply the 'opposite' technique. For example, if you are sick and you want health, cease thinking about illness and start thinking of health. Whatever enters your life is but the material expression of your belief. The idea of thinking 'opposite' is to steer your mind from the negative to the affirmative: from sickness to health, from misery to happiness, from poverty to abundance. Build up a case for what you *desire* and expunge from your mind thoughts and ideas of what you do *not* want.

If you are feeling pain you will only increase the feeling by telling yourself, 'I feel awful. I'm in pain'. The more you repeat this to your subconscious the more it will accept it as a command and produce what you really don't want. If you seek health, keep repeating the affirmation: 'I am healthy. My mind and body are in perfect harmony. I feel exuberant'.

Refrain from looking back over your shoulder and saying: 'It isn't working, the pain is still there'. If you think good thoughts in the morning and negative ones in the afternoon, you'll defeat the principle. Discipline the mind to think affirmatively *all* day, *every* day. Keep thinking in terms of what you want and how you wish to feel. Refrain from using words that represent a negative state, i.e.: headache, backache, pain, soreness, sickness, trouble, etc. Inject such words as: health, perfection, happiness, joy, peace, harmony, love, beauty, etc.

It is your duty to be healthy. If you want to attain health and *retain* it, get into the habit of thinking health and believing what you think. Set up a health consciousness pattern to free yourself from psychosomatic illnesses.

HOW TO STAY OUT OF HOSPITAL BEDS. Problems are inherent in today's living. Those unable to cope with their problems are filling hospital beds at an alarming rate. Man is yet to arrive at a suitable means whereby he is able to throw off his 'troubles' and live free of abnormal emotional stress and strain. The torment of worry is more and more leading to serious illnesses.

Man tends to dwell on the inequalities and negations of thinking and living and in so doing, has not or does not learn how to 'live'. Problems take over man instead of man taking over his problems and rationalizing towards solution and satisfaction.

Man's extended life span gives further time for fretting and worrying. The ulcer is fast becoming a symbol or badge of office of those who are unable to cope with their problems.

If man is to stay out of hospital beds he must learn to think clearly and objectively and to adjust mentally to the world around him. Maturity is achieved mentally and spiritually by using 'intelligence' in negating the negatives so that these attitudes do not come through and spoil life.

Man is a victim of his moods. Therefore, 'attitudes' are important in dispelling emotional ills. When man 'thinks' right, he 'acts' right. When wrong thinking causes wrong actions, emotional illness is brought about, which in turn manifests physical illness.

More than ever before young men are dying from heart attacks. They are unable to handle problems. If man would get to know and diligently apply the principle of *mind power* he would experience considerably less mental and physical illness and failure.

EMOTIONAL AND PHYSICAL ILLS BROUGHT ABOUT BY WORRY. Your doctor knows that approximately 85-per cent of all physical illnesses originate in the mind. When the mind is healthy the body follows suit. Those who suffer from psychosomatic illnesses may get temporary relief from patent medicines but seldom experience a permanent cure until the mind is cleansed and purified. *Your life is what your thoughts make it*. Poor problem solving creates a multitude of emotional responses setting off physical reactions in the body.

*Worry produces:*

depression
irritability
guilt feelings
anxiety
fear

*Which in turn brings:*

tension
headache
backache
nausea
insomnia
constipation
weight loss or gain
fatigue

**CONQUER WORRY AND ESCAPE FROM THE PRISON OF YOUR MIND.** You are not born with the worry habit; you acquire it. Worry is the most destructive of all human disease. The word comes from an Anglo-Saxon word meaning to *choke*. The majority of emotional ills are caused by frustration, anxiety and worry, brought about by fear and ignorance. The thinking processes are 'strangled' and rendered useless by their own doing. A person who is fearful is a prisoner of his own mind. He wallows in the trough of his mind rendering his conscious power inoperable because of sick, frustrated and confused thoughts. This 'state of mind' leaves the individual a mental and physical wreck.

'The greatest torture in the world for most people is to think,' said Luther Burbank. People who do not learn how to 'think', who allow a negative consciousness pattern to rule them, become emotional cripples who turn to alcohol or drugs to escape the reality of their negative existence.

It is impossible to hide from life. You *are* life. Some people think that by moving from one city to another they can leave their problems, worries and fears behind. This is 'escapism' and it is irrational thinking. The trouble with the 'get away from it all' attitude is that situations repeat themselves in the new environment. Problems become your co-pilot when you seek to fly away from them. The only place to find peace is *within*. It is not to be found in a far-off city, by hiding in a dark corner or in the taking of drugs or alcohol.

Alcoholism and drug taking are an admission that man cannot solve his problems. The aim of this book is to help people cope with their problems by applying certain rules of life that transform thinking habits and bring harmony and peace of mind. It amounts to thinking according to principle—*thinking up* instead of down.

You can escape from the prison of worry, fear, anxiety, frustration by using the power of your mind in an intelligent manner. *Learn to think affirmatively.* When worry begins to upset you, know that your subconscious mind already has the answer to your problem and will give it to you when you relax and think quietly and rationally about it. Ask: 'What is there I can intelligently respond to and constructively do?' Don't be anxious, don't cloud your mind with a dozen answers; take each step quietly and confidently and the worry will dissolve as the answer to your problem is revealed. Don't indulge in negative thoughts. With some people this is a way of life. If you allow yourself to partake of negative ideas and let them affect you emotionally, you can effectively eradicate them by constructive thinking. Bring into your mind all that is *good*. Believe in the power of healthy, affirmative thoughts and in what constructive thinking can accomplish for you. Your thoughts are a mighty force capable of bringing health, happiness and prosperity.

**HOW TO AVOID THE BLUES.** Mental depression or the 'blues' as it is commonly known, is sometimes more difficult to treat than the rarest disease. Depression is both a symptom and a disease. It accounts for more than half of the suicides that occur in the world each year.

Whether mild, severe or extreme, mental depression seriously damages self-esteem and health. Depression is brought about in many ways. It sometimes comes in the form of a blow to the ego of an individual when socially rejected. Examples are: A young man is rejected by a girl he seeks to take out. A salesman does badly at his work because his customers do not like his personality. A wife loses the attention of her husband. An elderly man is forced to retire from his job because he is being replaced by a younger man. All are examples of pride being hurt and giving rise to subsequent fits of depression.

Some individuals give the impression of being physically ill, even though there is no evidence of this upon examination by a doctor. Depression affects the rich and the poor alike. Kings and paupers are susceptible to it. Some of the symptoms of depression are:

> helplessness
> sadness
> feelings of guilt
> boredom
> loneliness (both a cause and a result of depression)
> insecurity
> inferiority
> nervousness
> lack of vitality (generally a mask for depression)

The most effective treatment is to dissolve the immediate cause of the depression. Sometimes a change in environment will help, although a vacation 'away from it all' is generally a temporary remedy and not always a final cure, but it helps. Rest, proper diet, a genuine interest in something, stepped up mental and physical activity, the taking on of new challenges such as: meeting new friends, changing jobs, a hobby, becoming interested in other people and centring the attention away from 'self', are all ways to beat depression. Above all, cease feeling sorry for yourself. I have a card I always carry with me which reads:

*A minute spent feeling sorry for myself is a minute totally wasted.*

When you feel depression coming on, reverse your thoughts and immediately get busy on some project and aim your thoughts at it. When you know how to regulate your thoughts and feelings, you have learned the secret of self-mastery and you are then able to enjoy personal power, happiness, peace of mind and excellent health.

**STARTLING FACTS ABOUT SUICIDE.** The unhappy young wife scrawled a note to her husband, took an overdose of sleeping pills and composed herself on the bed. 'Here at last will be peace and serenity', she thought as blackness swept over her.

Fortunately, her husband came home early and she was rushed to hospital and saved. Was this an attempt to escape from the problems of life? Did the young girl really want to die, or was she reaching out with a cry of 'Help me!'? Most experts on suicide agree that the aims of those attempting to commit suicide are really dramatic attempts to get others to help them. It is known that single people are far more prone to commit suicide than married people, that one is most likely to attempt it and fail, before the age of thirty five, and to succeed after the age of fifty.

Professional men and women, top executives and artists, commit suicide more than other people. It is interesting to note that in the U.S., according to an essay on suicide by *Time* magazine, there is a high rate of suicide among psychiatrists.

As much as one might think of poverty, love or poor health as being the major causes of suicide, these reasons are far from it. Poverty does not drive people to suicide; it is the wealthy whose fortunes are taken from them that are inclined to it. Seldom do people kill themselves because of a broken heart. And people who are physically ill rarely seek a way out by self-destruction.

Psychologists believe that most suicides want to be rescued. Freud noted, that suicide, more often than not, is designed to punish others or to try and manipulate them. 'The subconscious does not believe in its own death,' said Freud.

There is no situation that could ever confront you that cannot be solved. Life takes on real meaning when you set values for yourself, regard yourself as worthwhile and elevate your thoughts to the things that are of God — *Good*. There is a *Higher Power*. Turn to it and use it; it is yours for the asking.

**SET UP A BUFFER AGAINST CRISIS.** Many breakdowns in mental health occur at or following times of crisis, some of which are: puberty, marriage, birth of off-spring or siblings, death or separation from a loved one. A move from one city to another can be a crisis period, particularly for older people. Retirement is another crisis period; one is cut off from everyday routines and familiar faces and is faced with a new way of life, which, if not planned for, can lead to a breakdown in mental health. Look out for crisis periods. Prepare yourself for them emotionally by knowing that *all* situations eventually change and generally improve.

Turn a crisis into an advantage. Redirect your life, pick up the threads and enjoy a new set of friends, circumstances and environment.

Meet a crisis head on, face up to it and conquer it with sheer courage and faith in the right outcome.

CONTROL ANGER AND STEM EMOTIONAL ILLNESS. Chances are, if you don't get angry, *ever*, then you are a ready made case for a mental asylum. To get angry occasionally is natural. It is an emotional release necessary for normal health and happiness. The only problem with anger, is that many people let it get out of hand. Unchecked anger turns to violence which in turn brings destruction. During fits of rage, individuals become 'out of balance' and are apt to maim or kill others. Good seldom comes from unchecked anger.

We find it easy to excuse anger in ourselves, but difficult to tolerate anger in others. Anger, like a disease, can infect and fester in the form of grudges, jealousy, hatred. When this occurs, the only antidote is *forgiveness*. Be willing to forgive and forget. Cleanse your mind and heart. Turn hate into love. You owe your fellow man *love*—and that's all you owe him.

Change your aggressive nature into a peaceable nature and never allow anger to go beyond a certain limit so that it has an opportunity of doing yourself and others harm. Your degree of aggressive impulses and your ability to handle them realistically, has a more important role in maintaining health than you might realize.

MARITAL SQUABBLES BRING ILLNESSES. Husbands and wives who constantly quarrel are setting themselves up for ulcers, arthritis, insomnia, nervous tension, headaches and of course, possible divorce. A definite link between mental and physical ailments and hostility in marriage has been found in a study by a research team at the University of Michigan. Where there is resentment, anger and constant friction in a marriage, both husband and wife are letting themselves in for bouts of moodiness, depression and ill-health.

If you find that you are always depressed, constantly snapping and snarling at others and generally 'out of sorts', then you are harbouring a negative thought pattern, having cut off the flow of positive, pure, harmonizing thoughts. When you allow yourself to become irritated by another person and cannot adjust to the situation at hand, sooner or later a physical ailment will manifest from your attitude. Rule: *Alter your thoughts and keep them affirmative.*

CAPTURE INNER SERENITY WITH THE 5-MINUTE VACATION TECHNIQUE. Man has become far too busy building up anxieties and tensions, seldom allowing his mind enough time to rest. Loss of vital energy and a general 'run down' feeling are the result.

If you are tired of struggling through life worrying and fretting, being lonely and depressed, then you can overcome these negative mental states by regularly setting aside five minutes of each day to establish inner serenity. There is a deep need within us all to rest the mind and repose in tranquillity.

Far too much time is spent rushing about being nervous, impatient, intolerant and irritable. This surely makes life unhappy and dreary for those who are guilty of it.

Select your own time each day to visualize in your mind's eye the *beauty* of life. Make it your private five minute vacation time. Wherever you are, cease what you are doing, sit or lie down, close off thoughts of business or of your family and picture a green peaceful meadow or wooded hillside far removed from people and the noise of the city. Wander through your vacation resort and take in the natural beauty; hear the mellow sounds of the birds, the running stream; see the soft puffs of clouds, the blue sky, the shadows on the mountains. Your mental five minute vacation will slow you down, quiet your mind and give you a chance to recharge run down energy cells. Repeat your mental picture when you retire each night, it will help to bring on sleep.

BE HAPPY AND YOU'LL BE HEALTHY. Happiness is conducive to good health. Happy people are healthy people and healthy people are happy people. Happiness is a state of mind brought about by practicing healthy affirmative thoughts. When thoughts are of a negative nature you cannot be in a happy frame of mind. It would be fairly accurate to state that when you are in an unhappy state of mind you are also experiencing poor health.

Many people live their lives on the deferred payment plan. They expect a future occurrence or some person to come along and give them happiness. No one but *you* decrees how happy or unhappy you are to be. If you wait for a future event or person to come along to bring you life's greatest gift, you will be disappointed. *Happiness is internal.* It is produced by affirmative thoughts, ideas and feelings. You can be as happy or as unhappy as you desire. 'People are as happy as they make up their minds to be,' said Abraham Lincoln.

A state of happiness is necessary if you wish to experience well-being. The word disease means a state of unhappiness—*dis-ease*. Unhappiness is the cause of most psychosomatic illnesses. Happiness is the only lasting cure. You become happy by neutralizing all negative thoughts festering in your mind. The mind is the operator of the body and should not be allowed to become a slave to the whims of the body. Only *you* can determine how your mind is to work. If you allow it to become troubled and react negatively to petty annoyances, if you lose faith in yourself, feel lonely, distressed, sorry for yourself, then you are creating your own pattern of unhappiness and setting yourself up for physical illnesses. Happiness is a natural state and therefore it should be experienced far more times than an unhappy or unnatural state. It may not be possible to be happy all the time, but you should make up your mind to be happy *most* of the time.

Dr Norman Vincent Peale points out that every individual is in the manufacturing business and should 'manufacture happiness'. Happy people are healthier than unhappy people. Marriages are more successful when both husband and wife are happy. Cheerful businessmen are more successful than pessimistic ones. When you are happy you think better, look better, perform better, taste better, smell better, see better, hear and feel better. A state of happiness relaxes the mind and body. Stomach, liver, heart, indeed all internal organs function better when you are happy.

All religions prescribe happiness as a means of achieving the 'good life'. I have been unable to find anywhere in the scriptures, any message that decrees unhappiness, loneliness or sickness as a natural state for man.

Practise happy thinking and release yourself from distorted thinking principles that draw unhappiness to you. Reduce the pressures of worry, fear, anxiety, frustration and loneliness before they have an opportunity of bringing about emotional and physical illnesses. It is a good idea to list your worries, problems and fears. Take a good look at them. Know that you have the capacity to overcome all problems that may arise. Happiness and good health go hand in hand. Make up your mind to capture and keep the happiness habit by practising happy thinking.

MOST CRIMINALS COME FROM UNHAPPY HOMES. Harvard psychologists recently studied the correlation between happiness and criminality and concluded that 'happy people are seldom wicked people'. The study revealed that the majority of criminals in the United States were from unhappy homes.

LAUGHTER IS THE WORLD'S GREATEST MEDICINE. Become aware of the possibilities of a balanced sense of humour as a means of throwing off tensions and anxieties. Laughter is a healthy exertion. It breaks the gloom of depression. Doctors call it 'the world's best medicine'. It contains no drugs and it is absolutely free. Laughter brings harmony, peace and joy to your mind and body. Generous doses of laughter throughout your day are an important key to mental health. You will avoid mental illness by learning to adjust, by learning to be happy and by learning to laugh.

The next time you are confronted with a problem, try to see the funny side of it. Suggest to your subconscious mind an amusing outcome. Picture yourself in a situation connected with your problem dressed in an outlandish and funny way. This sets the subconscious on a positive vibration and pretty soon the enormity of your problem reduces itself to its proper perspective and your mind is open to work out a solution logically.

When you feel depressed and out of sorts, pause and read the comics. Charles Shultz's 'Peanuts' is worth a few moments reading of everyone's time. Besides its humour, it generally carries a message worth thinking about. Force yourself to smile, even if you have to look into a mirror to do it.

**COPY RUDYARD KIPLING'S SENSE OF HUMOUR.** Kipling had a keen sense of humour. The great writer once received a letter from a prospective buyer of his work. It read: 'I understand you are retailing literature at one dollar a word. I enclose one dollar, please send me a sample.'

The man who penned 'Gunga Din' kept the dollar and wrote back one word—'Thanks'. Capture the humour of Rudyard Kipling. Learn to apply humour to your daily living. Laugh and laugh often, you'll be suprised at how happy and healthy you will become.

**VITAMIN PILLS (AND HUMOUR) THE SECRET OF 94-YEAR-OLD'S HEALTH.** One of the most enjoyable interviews I have conducted on television was with a youthful-looking gentleman who was celebrating his ninety-fourth birthday. I asked him to what he attributed his longevity. 'Vitamin pills', he replied. 'How long have you been taking them?' I asked. 'Since I was ninety three,' came the reply. The gentleman was 'old' according to the calendar, but not according to his outlook on life. Don't take life too seriously. It has its lighter side. Apply the whimsy of my 94-year-old friend who still looks at life with a twinkle in his eye.

**SPIRITUAL HEALING.** To Infinite Intelligence, there is no incurable disease. Disease is largely a state of mind and when we deal with Universal Principle there is no limit to its healing power. All healing emanates from the hand of God and takes place through man's conscious and subconscious mind.

With spiritual healing it is important to commence with the premise that God is perfect, and that man is perfect because man is made in the image of God. Because man has strayed from God he has introduced imperfection into his life by his own choice.

Whenever praying for a healing, remove all doubt and fear or you will only succeed in negating that which you are praying for. Spiritual healing—calling on God and God-centred, not man-centred—can bring wonderful results when you remove the element of doubt and turn over your requests to a Higher Power. With pure mind, allow the healing currents of Life to flow through you as peace, joy, harmony and perfect health.

The late Dr Ernest Holmes, one of the great spiritual leaders of this century and author of a most inspiring book, **The Science of Mind,**\*

---

\***The Science of Mind.** Ernest Holmes, Dodd, Mead & Company, New York.

wrote: '. . . We feel that the spiritual or real man *is* perfect and we seek to uncover this perfection which is within every man's life. This is spiritual mind healing.' Dr Holmes, in his book, further indicates that: 'man will deliver himself from sickness and trouble in exact proportion to his discovery of himself and his true relationship to the Whole'.

Associate with the Whole. *Know* the truth, *feel* the truth and *express* the truth that you are made in the image of One who is Perfect and therefore, it is your right to enjoy peace, joy, harmony and perfect health.

### THE SPIRITUAL HEALINGS OF PHINEAS PARKHURST QUIMBY.
Phineas Parkhurst Quimby, a semi invalid of Belfast, Maine, was a pioneer in mental and spiritual healing around the 1830's and 1840's. Quimby used the principle of affirmative repetition to cure his own physical affliction. A self-educated man, he spent many hours attending esoteric lectures on spiritualism, mesmerism and various other psychological ideas of the times.

### MARY·BAKER EDDY—A QUIMBY PATIENT.
Quimby became known around Portland, Maine, as a successful healer. He had strong powers of observation and reflection. He cultivated the power of affirmative thoughts after realizing that most of his patients were responding just as well to cheap remedies as to complicated and expensive ones. Quimby reasoned that it was not so much the remedies that cured but the patients' 'belief' in the remedies.

One of Quimby's most famous patients was Mary Baker Eddy, founder of the Christian Science Church and herself an invalid. In 1862, she went to Portland to meet the great healer. Quimby cured her and she became his disciple, reading his notes and spreading his reputation. Quimby died in 1866 and a month later Mrs Eddy (then Mrs Patterson; she married Asa Gilbert Eddy in 1877 after divorcing Dr Daniel Patterson), again fell ill and a helpless cripple. After more than 10 years of living in poverty and loneliness, Mrs Patterson, according to her memoirs, 'came upon' the 'Science of Divine Healing', and cured herself.

Quimby's technique was to teach sick people that affirmative thoughts held in the mind and believed to be true, dissolved negative opposition and allowed the healing currents to flow through the body and restore health. It was the power of 'suggestion' through the spoken word that healed. *The Quimby Manuscripts*, published in 1921 by Thomas Y. Crowell, New York City, give newspaper accounts of Quimby's treatments and miraculous cures of the sick.

### ESTABLISH FAITH IN YOUR RECOVERY.
Doctors often express the view that patients who have faith in their recovery, stand a better chance of surviving serious illnesses or major operations than those who are sceptical or who have given up hope. The ability to 'fight back',

is a necessary one. Feelings of courage and strength could pull you through where feelings of helplessness and despair might not. Attitudes of faith, hope and enthusiasm for complete recovery bring it about much sooner. *Thy faith have made thee whole.*—MATT. 9.22.

## SUMMARY OF IDEAS TO HELP YOU ATTAIN MENTAL WELL BEING

1. *Your mental outlook can make you ill or healthy. 'Right' attitudes are essential to good health. Healthy thoughts produce a healthy mind and body.*

2. *Use the 'opposite' technique. Think in terms of what you want and not what your present condition is.*

3. *You are going to run into problems. It's what you* **do** *about them that counts. Learn to rationalize problems and you'll stay out of hospital beds.*

4. *To avoid worry and fear which bring about mental depression, regulate your thoughts, centre attention away from yourself. Get interested in others. Get active. Reverse all negative thoughts. Substitute affirmative thoughts.*

5. *To get angry occasionally is natural. Do not allow anger to get the upper hand. Practise forgiveness.*

6. *Avoid marital and family squabbles. Practise love, joy, peace and goodwill.*

7. *To capture peace of mind take 'five-minute vacations'—relax, picture a tranquil setting. Give yourself time to recharge run down energy cells.*

8. *Happiness is conducive to health. Happy people are healthy people.*

9. *It is chemically impossible for your body to produce ulcers while you are laughing. Learn to laugh and* **often.**

10. *To Infinite Intelligence there is no incurable disease. All healing emanates from the hand of God through the mind.*

# HOW TO ATTAIN
# PHYSICAL WELL BEING

## Success Ideas in this Chapter

- What You Eat Today Influences Your Health Tomorrow
- What To Eat For Health And Energy
- What NOT To Eat
- Boil Bake Or Grill But Never Fry
- Ailments Brought About By Nutritional Deficiences
- Don't Eat When You Are Angry Unless You Want Indigestion And Ulcers
- Avoid Overweight
- How To Avoid Backache
- How To Avoid Ulcers
- Edmond Samuel's Advice To Stem Ulcers
- How To Avoid A Heart Attack
- Actors Know The Importance Of A Relaxed Performance
- 6 Techniques To Relax And Throw Off Tension
- Jim Became A Top Salesman When He Learned To Avoid Stress
- 162-Year-Old Russian Still Climbing Mountains
- How To Beat Insomnia
- 10 Sleep Techniques
- Proper Rest Is Important To Health But Too Much Sleep Is Dangerous
- Avoid Headache, Nausea And Energy Loss Brought About By Eye Strain
- It Sounds Silly But Play The Fool
- Simple Exercises To Relax The Eyes
- Overcome That TIRED Feeling And Put Zest In Your Life
- Don't Sit Moaning—Take Action
- LOVE What You Are Doing
- Trio Of Famous Actresses Conserve Energy
- Summary Of Ideas To Help You Attain Physical Well Being

# 13

*Think of the ills from which you are exempt, and it will aid you to bear patiently those which now you may suffer.*

CECIL

**WHAT YOU EAT TODAY INFLUENCES YOUR HEALTH TOMORROW.** It will pay you to keep fit, to build muscle, increase blood circulation and to keep veins and arteries active and healthy. If you insist on eating like a horse you may end up with about the same life span. Overweight people are unhealthy people. Proper diet helps to prolong life. Your energy and good looks are dependent upon the state of your physical health, which in turn is reliant upon the kind of food you eat. By carefully selecting what you eat you can gain energy, renew your body and remain younger, longer.

You will feel better mentally and physically if you stay away from starches and sugars. Carbohydrates are high in calories and result in overweight, listlessness and heart problems. Protein is your best friend. It prevents disease and nourishes your body and gives you energy. If you are nervous and tense, chances are your body is craving vitamins and minerals.

**TV STAR KNOWS VALUE OF PROPER FOODS.** One of the main causes of poor health is artificial, processed and chemicalized foods which cannot be easily assimilated or eliminated by the body. They remain there and cause malfunctioning of organs. It is therefore, advisable to eat fresh foods.

Film and T.V. actor Bob Cummings, maintains it is the food we eat that gives us 'good looks and vitality'. And Cummings is a perfect

185

example of what eating 'good' food can accomplish in the appearance department.

### WHAT TO EAT FOR HEALTH AND ENERGY

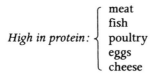

High in protein: {
 meat
 fish
 poultry
 eggs
 cheese
}

Vitamins and minerals: {
 most fruits
 vegetables
 honey
 cereals
 100% wholemeal and rye breads
}

### WHAT NOT TO EAT

ham (fatty meats)
cream soups
gravies
refined sugars
cream puddings
rich pastries
pies
garlic bread
white bread
mayonnaise

**BOIL, BAKE OR GRILL BUT NEVER FRY.** I am surprised at the amounts of fried foods most Australians and Britishers eat. Meat, fish, poultry and potatoes saturated in repulsive hot fat. Food cooked this way is unfit for the lowest animal to digest, let alone the sensitive stomach of a human. If you want to avoid heart problems and enjoy better health and longer life, don't eat fatty foods. Boil, bake or grill meats, fish and poultry—*never fry.*

Don't boil the life out of fresh vegetables—*steam* them. *Don't* fill up on white bread, rich pastries and highly sugared tea or coffee. Use honey to sweeten beverages.

**AILMENTS BROUGHT ABOUT BY NUTRITIONAL DEFI-CIENCIES.** When you starve your body of the right foods you are denying yourself clear skin, healthy hair, shining eyes, vitality and an alert mind. Make sure your diet is *growth* promoting. The following ailments have been traced to nutritional deficiencies:

| | |
|---|---|
| HEADACHES | ULCERS |
| NERVOUSNESS | COLDS |
| TIREDNESS | SKIN DISORDERS |
| TENSION | BACKACHE |
| POOR CIRCULATION | CONSTIPATION |
| HIGH BLOOD PRESSURE | INDIGESTION |
| POOR EYESIGHT | HEART TROUBLE |
| LIVER TROUBLE | INSOMNIA |

**DON'T EAT WHEN YOU ARE ANGRY UNLESS YOU WANT INDIGESTION AND ULCERS.** Before sitting down to a meal it is customary to cleanse the hands. I would add another requisite: cleanse the mind of all anger, resentment, hostility and ugly thoughts. If you eat while emotionally upset, food turns sour, as the intestines are unable to properly digest food while the stomach organs are tense.

Clear your mind completely of all negative thoughts. If you are mad at someone or something or have problems, forget them while you are consuming food. You'll enjoy your meals more and get to eat more of them by relaxing your mind and stomach when you eat.

**AVOID OVERWEIGHT.** Don't starve yourself. Eat healthy amounts of food, but make sure the food you do eat is good food and low in calories. Pocket books listing foods and their calorie content are available. Purchase one and get to know the foods that are low in calories. Stay off fried foods if you want to lose weight.

Be active. Exercise as often as possible to tone up muscles. Exercise also burns up the calories you take in as food. Take long jogs and brisk walks. When you walk you take in three times as much air as when you are stationary. Take the occasional steam bath. This helps to purify the body of toxins and accumulated grime which become embedded in the pores of the skin.

**HOW TO AVOID BACKACHE.** A lot of backaches are caused by lying in a soft chair for long periods while watching television or reading. This puts a strain on the middle of the spine and hampers circulation to it. This causes the tissues and the intervertebral discs to break down. The main vertebrae then rub against each other through the collapsed discs.

Two thirds of all backaches are caused by poor posture. If you want to avoid backache, practise good posture. Sit up straight, don't slouch, stand erect with shoulders back.

Mild exercise in the form of walking is often an excellent way of getting relief from lower back pains. Hot baths, massages and heat treatments are others.


**HOW TO AVOID ULCERS.** Ulcers affect approximately one in every ten people. Ulcers are brought about by worry, anger, hostility, resentment, fatigue, fatty fried foods, an excessive use of cigarettes and alcohol and lack of tension-breaking exercise.

Don't keep your problems bottled up. Release them; talk them over with those who may be able to help you find a solution to them. Whenever you feel tension creeping on, stop what you are doing and relax. Don't physically push yourself without a breather. Leave your problems at work. Never take them home with you. Do not allow others to get you fighting mad. When you get mad you increase acid secretion. When you are happy and laughing it is chemically impossible for your body to produce ulcers. Remember: *laugh often,* it relieves tension and keeps you healthy.

Scientists believe that by taking prescribed amounts of vitamin U ulcers are kept in check. A further remedy for those already suffering with ulcers is to drink small amounts of strained, boiled cabbage juice. If you suspect that you have an ulcer, see your doctor. Pains of any description are warning signs. *An ounce of prevention is better than a pound of cure.*


**EDMOND SAMUELS' ADVICE TO STEM ULCERS.** One of the most unique services ever devised for those suffering from tension and headache was Edmond Samuels' Headache Bar in Sydney. The menu, a list of concoctions for the remedy of minor aches and pains, carried a clever piece of philosophy: *Placidity prevents acidity.* In other words DON'T GET DISTURBED. Placidity is inner harmony. When achieved, it conserves energy and prevents sickness.

Edmond, a former chemist, is now a prominent Sydney entrepreneur and manager of theatrical talent and an individual with an excellent mental outlook on life.


**HOW TO AVOID A HEART ATTACK.** Heart disease is a greater killer in Australia than in most countries. The reason: indolence, wrong foods, tension. Medical specialists believe that heart disease can be prevented from attacking the middle-aged by doing something about it during the teenage years. Coronary heart disease affects those who drive themselves too hard in everything they attempt to do. The rule: *moderation in everything.*

Doctors are sure that fatty foods, high blood pressure, lack of exercise, smoking and drinking to excess, emotional stress and fatigue, all contribute to heart disease. It will do you little good in the long run, to drive yourself to success and have a heart attack on the way. Follow the eight precautionary measures and you could well avoid heart disease.

1. Get plenty of rest
2. Exercise regularly
3. Avoid getting tense, angry, hostile
4. Don't smoke or drink to excess
5. Avoid excess weight
6. Control high blood pressure
7. Avoid fried, fatty foods (check your diet)
8. Get regular medical check ups

**ACTORS KNOW THE IMPORTANCE OF A RELAXED PERFORMANCE.** Tension and worry cause you to age quicker than anything else. Nervous tension robs you of the joys and pleasures of a happy and healthy life. Many performers I know have yet to learn the secret of an enthusiastic, yet *relaxed* performance. I have watched them backstage tied up in knots, chain smoking, fidgeting, while waiting their turn to perform. Tension, anxiety, stress and strain impair a good performance and bring about physical illnesses.

Being keyed up and tense before an important event is different from being alert and enthusiastic. The former stands out, causes others to notice your insecurity. The latter impresses others who see you as calm, poised and confident.

I have seen a few performers become quite ill prior to a performance. I have watched others, physically relaxed—though mentally alert and on their toes—give brilliant performances. Frank Sinatra, Dean Martin, Bing Crosby, Pat Boone, Billy Daniels, Bob Hope, Phyllis Diller, Billy Eckstein, Henry Fonda, Wayne Newton, Nancy Sinatra, to mention a few, know the importance of a 'relaxed' performance, free from tension and strain.

**6 TECHNIQUES TO RELAX AND THROW OFF TENSION.** Eastern mystics have such control over their bodies they feel no pain. Their secret is: shed tension, relax, gain control over the body by controlling the mind. If you are tense, relax by directing your full attention to your muscles and commanding them to 'let go'. Take five minutes of each day to apply the following techniques to release tension and strain and bring about complete mental and physical relaxation.

# PROGRESSIVE BODY RELAXATION

1. Relax the eyes, then the eyebrows, then the forehead. Let the jaw drop, now release all tension from the neck, the shoulders, the left arm followed by the right arm. Feel the tension go from the hand and from the fingers. Relax the stomach muscles. Now release tension from the right leg and toes, then the left leg and toes. Repeat the word 'relax' over and over. Feel every inch of your body releasing tension.

2. Imagine you are lying on a huge, soft pillow, resting on a cloud which is drifting in space. You are weightless and your body feels light and free and completely relaxed.

3. Take long, slow, deep breaths while lying down. Exhale slowly. (This is an excellent technique for getting rid of butterflies in the stomach which may crop up prior to an important speech, introduction or event.)

4. Soak in a hot tub and repeat technique 1.

5. To take tension knots out of the neck, lift the shoulders as high as possible, hold the position for ten seconds then release. Repeat ten times. Relax the arms, hands and face. Allow the jaw to drop.

6. Take a long, brisk walk. It will tire and at the same time relax you. (Dr Billy Graham throws off tension by taking jogs and brisk walks, during busy crusade schedules.)

**JIM BECAME A TOP SALESMAN WHEN HE LEARNED TO AVOID STRESS.** A young salesman—call him Jim Downes—was fired from his job because several customers had complained to the sales manager that Jim was often irritable and rude when taking orders.

I hired Jim to work on my newspapers as an advertising space salesman. It wasn't too long before complaints began coming in about his rudeness. I liked Jim. He was really a pleasant fellow at heart. Instead of firing him I took him to lunch to see if I could find out the reason for his abrupt, irritable and sometimes rude manner. As we chatted, I discovered that he was spending long hours every night on a self improvement course. He had set a goal of reading five books a week on memory training, salesmanship, human relations and general knowledge. Jim's intentions were good but his methods were self-defeating. Each night he would pour over literature anxious to keep up with the hectic schedule he had set for himself. Jim over-taxed himself, became keyed up, strained and nervous. In addition to this, he was averaging only five hours of sleep a night. Any wonder his nerves jumped during the day and his manner was irritable and rude.

I suggested to Jim that he set up a new schedule; that he reduce his reading periods to one hour at a time, get up, move around, take a walk, do something else for a short period, then resume reading. This would give his mind time to absorb all that he had read and the break would allow him to physically and mentally relax. In short: regulate, relax and avoid stress and strain.

Jim regulated his time efficiently, learned to accomplish things without tension and today, is a top sales executive in Canada.

**162-YEAR-OLD RUSSIAN STILL CLIMBING MOUNTAINS.** Whatever the secret of longevity is, several Russians living in the hill towns and villages of the remote Soviet Caucasus seem to have discovered it. The grandaddy of the group is Shirali Mislimov, 162 years of age, who still chops wood and climbs mountain trails for exercise. Beim Makhraliyeva, 135, is the chief baby sitter for a village, whose residents have an average age of eighty five.

The Russians maintain there are more than 5,000 persons who claim to have lived more than a century. According to Soviet doctors who have studied the groups, outdoor living, regular work, lack of tension, wholesome food and plenty of fresh air are the secrets of long life. While you might not live too far beyond the century mark, you can enjoy extra years by following the pattern of tension-free living experienced by the Russians.

**HOW TO BEAT INSOMNIA.** If your toss and turn and find it difficult to get a good night's sleep, the safest method is to get up and do mild exercise. Stay away from drugs of any description, they offer only temporary relief and will not solve your problem of insomnia. Try the following techniques to attain restful, health-building slumber.

# TEN SLEEP TECHNIQUES

1. Do mild forms of exercise before bed time.
2. Read light material.
3. Slow down all mental and physical activity one hour prior to retiring.
4. Take a warm bath.
5. Listen to soft, pleasant music.
6. Do not eat or drink before you retire (indigestion and a heavy stomach won't bring about sleep).
7. Never take problems to bed with you.
8. Still the wheels of your mind and repeat: 'I am drowsy. I feel sleep coming on'.
9. Hold pleasant tranquil thoughts: joy, peace, harmony, beauty. Picture a tranquil scene: mountains, pastures, etc.
10. RELAX body and mind, feel weightless, drift into sleep.

**PROPER REST IS IMPORTANT TO HEALTH BUT TOO MUCH SLEEP IS DANGEROUS.** People who sleep longer hours than are necessary have a higher death rate from heart attacks than those who are normal sleepers. Medical research has shown that the death rate from strokes was considerably higher among those who slept nine or ten hours a night than for people who averaged seven hours a night. The coronary death rate was also higher for those who were long sleepers. Among those who slept ten or more hours a night, the death rate was 286-per cent higher than for those who slept seven hours.

Sleep is important to health—normal amounts of sleep. For most people eight hours is sufficient.

**IT SOUNDS SILLY BUT PLAY THE FOOL.** When you are in pain make strange noises in rhythm with the pain. It helps to divide your attention and reduce some of the physical discomfort.

**AVOID HEADACHE, NAUSEA AND ENERGY LOSS BROUGHT ABOUT BY EYE STRAIN.** When the body is tense the eyes are tense. Tension causes eye strain and impairs vision. Eyes sap up large amounts of energy and when overworked, bring about headaches and nausea. When eyes lose their relaxation you become tense, irritable and fatigued.

Normal seeing is relaxed seeing. Defective vision makes the eyes stare instead of shifting rapidly. When staring eyes learn to shift and relax, vision is improved. Relaxation of the eyes and mind brings relaxation of the whole body, resulting in improved physical and mental health. Mental and physical relaxation results in relaxation of the eyes and when this occurs vision is better.

Thoughts of dishonesty and hate cause the eyes to be shifty, thoughts of fear make the eyes cloudy, thoughts of love, joy, harmony, make the eyes sparkle.

If you have poor vision, picture your eyes magically acquiring X-ray vision each time you remove your glasses. When your husband says he won't be home for dinner, use your x-ray vision to seek him out. If you should lose something in the house, remove your glasses and seek to find it with your x-ray vision. It sounds silly but it's been known to restore weakened eye muscles by suggesting to the subconscious that the eyes have enormous strength and the unusual ability to see what others can't.

### SIMPLE EXERCISES TO RELAX THE EYES

1. Roll the head clockwise five times then anti clockwise five times. Repeat until neck muscles feel free.

2. Close the eyelids, picture a small circle. Concentrate on the circle and follow the circumference clockwise ten times, then anti clockwise ten times, moving the head slowly. Repeat until strain is relieved.

3. Close the lids, cross the palms, gently hold the palms over the eyes for five minutes. The warmth and energy from the palms refreshes the eyes.

4. Close the lids, sit or lie down, place cold tea bags over the eyes for as long as possible.

5. Fix a position on a wall, blink at it twenty times, close the lids, move the head as far right as possible, then to the centre and again blink twenty times. Now turn the head as far left as possible and repeat the procedure ten times.

### OVERCOME THAT TIRED FEELING AND PUT ZEST IN YOUR LIFE.
You lose energy and become easily fatigued when life becomes dull in your mind. Your mind gets bored when it is denied challenges and is devoid of interests. Within your mind are unlimited resources for development. It is up to you to live constructively and creatively. Your life becomes more meaningful, zestful and happier when you keep your mind active and interested in your personal development.

Abundant energy is the first requirement for the full enjoyment of life. If you feel tired, listless, fatigued give yourself a mental boost by elevating your thoughts and substituting mental tranquillizers for bottled ones. Take charge of your mind and order it around. Tell it what you wish it to do and how you want to feel. Whatever you *impress* on your subconscious is eventually *expressed.*

Take an active interest in everything you come in contact with: people, places, things. Meet different people, go to different places. Get *enthusiastic* over people, places and things. When you meet a friend, don't save your enthusiasm, shower him with it. Make him feel you are really glad to see him. Watch his eyes and reactions to your friendliness. When you tackle a job, tackle it with enthusiasm—*like* what you do. Get genuinely interested and throw yourself into it with abandon. The more you love your work, the less time you will find to become bored and tired.

**DON'T SIT MOANING—TAKE ACTION.** While conducting a two-way radio program on a Sydney broadcasting station, I was continually called by people who complained about the Government, their families, things they disliked, taxes, wars and a dozen and one other things. Many people are quite content to sit and complain but never to do anything about the things that disturb them. Don't sit moaning about the state of your life—*do something about it.* Boredom and fatigue disappear when the basic need is fulfilled. The individual who is up and about doing something to enhance his existence is never tired and seldom ill. He doesn't have time to become tired because he's too busy 'living'.

*Find Life.* Set out each day with a definite plan of action to further your career, enhance your marriage, assist others less fortunate or to learn, progress and conquer.

**LOVE WHAT YOU ARE DOING.** While covering the Canadian elections as a journalist-broadcaster during the latter part of the 1950's, I had a first hand opportunity of watching Prime Minister John Diefenbaker fulfill exhausting campaign schedules and still remain fresh and energetic at the end of each day. 'How do you make so many speeches and appearances and not tire?' I asked him. 'Because I love what I'm doing and I have an opportunity of meeting so many interesting people,' was his reply.

Here's the secret: *love what you are doing. Take an interest in others and enjoy every phase of your job.*

**TRIO OF FAMOUS ACTRESSES CONSERVE ENERGY.** Working in a film studio can be tiring, both physically and mentally, as most motion picture and television performers know. Lucille Ball when asked by a reporter how she conserved energy, said: 'I budget my energies. I reserve and don't let things rip me apart at the wrong times. The most important thing is what I have to do at that moment.'

The secret: *Budget your energies. Give out a little at a time. Reserve. Concentrate on doing one thing at a time and give all your energy to that.*

Ginger Rogers fans will not be surprised to learn that the charm and beauty of this actress have changed little over the years. Miss Rogers' hobby is keeping fit and she is a walking testimonial of how youthful one can remain by following affirmative principles of living.

Miss Rogers believes that the thought of *age*, ages, which is the reason she leaves thoughts of the past behind, which is where they rightly belong. The secret of energy she feels, is: 'loving God and your fellow man. Those who carry resentment and hate make themselves ill. Ugly thoughts are ugly making, just as beautiful thoughts make beauty.'

The secret: *Don't hate, love.*

Mary Martin finds plenty of energy by sticking to her philosophy which is: 'not to attempt more than I can handle and to apply discipline, enthusiasm and moderation.'

The secret: *Regulate life. Apply discipline and do everything enthusiastically.*

# SUMMARY OF IDEAS TO HELP
# YOU ATTAIN PHYSICAL
# WELL BEING

1. *What you eat today influences your health tomorrow. Eat nourishing foods. Stay away from fatty foods. Boil, bake, or grill*—**never fry.**

2. *Do not eat when you are angry. Uncontrolled hostility at meal times turns food sour and brings ulcers and heart problems.*

3. *Tension and worry bring emotional and physical illnesses. Do relaxing exercises, take brisk walks. Get your mind off your work, your problems.*

4. *Follow the advice of Edmond Samuels;* **placidity prevents acidity.**

5. *Rest is important but* **too** *much rest is harmful. Regulate sleep.*

6. *Loss of energy is due to boredom and laziness. Take on challenges, new interests. Find life and live life. Enjoy life.*

7. *Conserve energy. Give out a little at a time. Apply discipline and do every job with love and enthusiasm.*

8. *You can avoid physical illnesses by right thinking, right eating and right living. Avoid stress and strain. Think health, not sickness. Take charge of your mind and your mind will take charge of your body.*

# HOW TO USE THE POWER OF PRAYER TO ATTAIN HAPPINESS AND FULFILMENT

*Success Ideas in this Chapter*

- The Golden Key To Happiness
- Prayer CHANGES Things
- The Amazing Power of Prayer
- How To Pray Effectively
- Love Is The Answer To Fear And Hate
- Relax When You Pray
- You Cannot Substitute Prayer For Stupidity
- He Came To Give THANKS To Lincoln
- Give Thanks To God
- Salesmen Tripled Their Income With This Prayer
- Meditation Is The Most Effective Tranquilizer
- How To Meditate
- Good Literature Helps To Expand The Mind
- The Best Seller Of All Time Should Be In Every Home
- The Golden Rule Is The Same In All Holy Books
- Summary Of Ideas To Attain Happiness And Fulfilment

# 14

*More things are wrought by prayer than the world dreams of. What are men better than sheep or goats, that nourish a blind life within the brain, if, knowing God, they lift no hands of prayer both for themselves and those who call them friends!*

TENNYSON

**THE GOLDEN KEY TO HAPPINESS.** The greatest powers of life are thought, speech and prayer. The key to successful living is the intelligent and sincere application of prayer. Prayer is a desire for right action to take place in your life and in the lives of others. It is a request for perfect circumstance. It is an opportunity to commune with God, to establish a relationship with God and to give thanks for the 'good' that has taken place in your life. When you pray, you establish a Oneness with God which is your primary objective on earth. Separation from God is the cause of all misery and failure.

Prayer is the most powerful form of energy that you can generate and it manifests your desires according to the *degree* of your faith. When you pray you take on a new mode of thinking, for you are thinking 'in harmony' with the harmonious thoughts of God—*all that is good.* Your views and disposition are transformed as you apply the truths of God to your daily life.

The application of prayer will bring into your life a greater intelligence, an ability to make wise decisions and a faculty for getting along with and understanding people. It will bring a clearer understanding of yourself and your role in life. It will help you to express your true religion, which is what you 'think' deep down, not necessarily what you profess.

It is God's will that you live your life experiencing health, happiness and prosperity. It is not the will of God that you live in a hovel and experience loneliness and misery, although man sometimes wrongly blames God for his mistakes and failures.

If there is 'lack' in your life, the application of prayer will bring a better awareness of God's love. It will bring a sense of security, helping you to meet your needs and giving you unlimited strength. Whatever the need, prayer is the answer. It is the key to happiness.

**PRAYER CHANGES THINGS.** Whenever you spend a quiet moment in silent prayer you change both soul and body for the better. It is not possible that any person could pray for a single instant and not get some good from it. 'No man ever prayed without learning something,' said Emerson.

The sincere application of prayer restores health, puts you on your feet and strengthens your sense of purpose. Above all, it restores self respect, if that has been lost.

God acts for you through your prayers. They should not be repeated requests for God to use His power, but rather, requests for guidance, wisdom, love, understanding, compassion, strength, appreciation and gratitude. Pray for assistance in planning your daily life and in your relationships with others.

Prayer is psychologically sound. It works when you release your inner feelings and commune with Divine Intelligence. Constant prayer gives you a feeling of well being, it brings an inner calm that completely changes the negative into the affirmative. Prayer will also give you an inner power to alter negative circumstance in your outer world and attract to you riches and prosperity.

**THE AMAZING POWER OF PRAYER.** I have heard many men and women tell amazing stories of how prayer—*sincere prayer*—has overcome personal and financial problems, supplied the wisdom to make agonizing decisions, healed broken marriages, given strength in times of personal loss, transformed the lives of alcoholics, drug addicts and criminals, and healed so called 'incurable' disease.

Prayer makes you strong, confident and poised. Somehow it makes you *different*. It works for me in my life and I have seen it work 'miraculously' in the lives of others. Prayer changes things if you pray without ceasing and with faith in the outcome. However, don't expect God to answer frivolous requests. He has equipped you with a mind with which to reason and you are expected to use it. Request the *wisdom* to steer your life in the direction you wish it to take and the *faith* to carry on, regardless of circumstance. *This is the confidence that we have in him, that, if we ask any thing according to his will, he heareth us.*—1 JOHN 5:14.

**HOW TO PRAY EFFECTIVELY.** Prayer is a personal thing. It is a way of opening your life to a stream of spiritual power. It is a time to enter the room of your mind, to offer up gratitude and to ask for the guidance of 'perfection' in your life and in the lives of others. Prayer is an admittance of your need of God.

The offering of prayer does not always necessitate attending a church or kneeling in solitude. Prayer can be offered in the quiet of your bedroom, while travelling to work in your car or public transport, while attending a function or at any convenient time while you are awake. Every spare moment of every day gives you the chance to offer prayers of 'thanks' for the 'good' that has entered your life. *In everything give thanks.* Pray for wholeness then picture wholeness in your mind. Shoot silent prayers out at people you come in contact with, particularly those who are antagonistic toward you. Pray for their good.

Whenever possible, seek a quiet corner away from others to pray and be illumined by the presence of God. Turn over your requests with faith. When you consciously love God and bless all that He has given you in your life, you will find added 'good' entering your domain. You will marvel at the inner peace and security prayer brings. It will surprise you that just 'thinking' about God in an affirmative way will attract to you the things you desire and bring countless unexpected blessings. Do not dwell on, 'how little I have'. Think in terms of 'how much is mine', and it will multiply.

**LOVE IS THE ANSWER TO FEAR AND HATE.** Never pray harbouring negative feelings of hate or fear. Negative feelings bring negative conditions. Discard negative thoughts and feelings from your consciousness and allow your heart to be filled with love, for it is the *law of love* that *love given is love received.* Prayers of love are the greatest prayers you can offer. They work like a magnet, attracting radiant, joyous and everlasting peace, that flows through your life like the gentle cascade of crystal waters.

*Perfect love casteth out fear.* Love dissipates hate and disolves fear, the two most common negative conditions that cause unhappiness and failure.

If you desire to be healthier, happier and more prosperous, if you want to get closer to God, then offer prayers of love; love for your family, your friends, your country and your fellow man. If you want to change your life, pray with love in your heart.

**RELAX WHEN YOU PRAY.** Many people strain and are tense when they pray. They attempt to use will power to bring results. Tension and will power are the natural enemies of prayer and are the major reasons prayers remain unanswered.

When you strain to receive an affirmative result by will power, you get nowhere. You cannot coerce God by demanding and begging for answers to your prayers. When you pray thinking, 'I must get an answer' or 'God must listen to me', you are using will power and you will not accomplish anything. Your prayers should not be continual demands for handouts from God. Effective prayer is not begging.

*Relax*, don't strain. Quiet the wheels of your mind and pray calmly and confidently, free from tension or fear. Free your heart of negative feelings, cleanse your mind of negative thoughts and harmonize your thoughts and feelings with the perfection and beauty of life. *God is the sum total of all that is perfect.* Dwell on this truth, know that God represents: love, truth, beauty, harmony, joy and goodness. Acknowledge these harmonious states as being yours for the asking. Accept that: *The Kingdom of God is within you.* Luke 17:21. Know it; affirm it; live with it.

### YOU CANNOT SUBSTITUTE PRAYER FOR STUPIDITY.

*Ye ask and receive not because ye ask amiss.* JAMES 4:3.

Many people seem to feel prayer is a substitution for commonsense and the application of wisdom. If you are praying for good health it is foolhardy to be careless about your eating, drinking, rest and exercise habits. If you pray for safety on the highways, prayer should not be substituted for careless driving habits. If you wish to pass exams, prayer is not going to get you through if you are lazy and neglect study. If you pray for marital happiness it is ridiculous to expect it if you are not faithful to your spouse. Prayer is not a substitution for laziness, stupidity or for repeatedly committing sin.

The scientific application of prayer works when your words and heart correspond and when you cease begging for selfish handouts. Prayer begins with honesty. It is the outpouring of the heart.

### HE CAME TO GIVE THANKS TO LINCOLN.
When Abraham Lincoln was in office as President, he was continually hounded by people wanting something from him to further their own careers. An old friend from his home town paid him a visit at the White House and the two chatted about their childhood. Lincoln asked his friend if there was anything he could do, as President, that might help him. 'Nothing, Mr President, I came here to renew an old friendship and to tell you that I believe in you and I pledge to you my support and loyalty. I give thanks for our friendship.' Lincoln clasped his friend's hand and exclaimed, 'You can't realise how much your words mean to me. You are the only man who has come to see me in Washington who hasn't begged me for something.'

### GIVE THANKS TO GOD.
Pray without begging and continually asking for things. Give genuine 'thanks' for what you already have and pray for the guidance and wisdom to make your own way in life. You have much to give thanks for: your job, health, freedom from tyranny, your friends and family and much more. Bless what you have and give genuine 'thanks' for it.

**SALESMEN TRIPLED THEIR INCOME WITH THIS PRAYER.**
A group of salesmen employed by a large American Insurance Company was given a prayer to repeat each morning prior to commencing work. Those who used it in a sincere way tripled their income and many reported selling 85-per cent of all prospects called on.

I BELIEVE I am always Divinely guided.

I BELIEVE I will always take the right turn of the road.

I BELIEVE God will always make a way where there is no way.

I BELIEVE with God *all things* are possible.

The prayer is a simple one, but honestly and conscientiously used it will enhance your life. Memorize it and repeat it often.


**MEDITATION IS THE MOST EFFECTIVE TRANQUILLIZER.**
Meditation is an individual thought process whereby man, using step by step methods of concentration, may consciously commune with God. Thinking is directed away from the need or problem and placed in alignment with the Mind of God. Through relaxed concentration, the attention is focused upon the Infinite, resulting in man receiving his highest good in the form of peace, joy, harmony, beauty, wisdom, security and wholeness. Meditation, above all else, is companionship with God.

The only way God can act through you is through your mind. When you open your mind to the Mind of God you allow new avenues of splendour to enter your life. God is *within* man and man is here to express all of the qualities of God. Meditation should not be thought of as simply concentration, particularly concentration on material things.

To meditate is to bring the mind to a focal point of concentration, allowing Divine energy to flow through it. To do so, is to experience the presence of God. The key to life is not somewhere outside of man. It is to be found within the realm of man's mind. The harmony and beauty of life is the expression of the presence of God. When man practises the presence of God, he is experiencing 'life' in its purest form.

Meditation is a ways and means of bringing our hearts, minds and souls into a consciousness of peace. It is the practice of inner renewal and refreshment. The subjects of meditation are the aspects of truth. There must be no strain, tension or effort on the part of those seeking quiet moments in meditation.

**HOW TO MEDITATE.** Spend 15 minutes early in the morning or late at night in a room where there is no chance of being disturbed. If possible, sit facing *east*, as one is better polarized (cosmic rays emanate from east to west). Sit comfortably and be still. Close the eyes and focus without strain upward to the centre of the forehead—the central point of spiritual energy. Have no strained concern for any thing, place or person. All problems are left behind in the outer world. Shut out all confusion and discord. 'Let go' things of the outer and quiet the wheels of the mind. Loosen your mind from the consciousness of body weight. Relax the muscles of the body and remain in a seemingly weightless position free from tension. Meditate on the thought: 'I am at peace. Tranquillity, harmony and wholeness are mine.' Meditate on the waves of tranquillity that roll through your being like the gentle swell of the sea. Drop your mind into the infinite well of your heart.

When you practise the presence of God you experience the presence of peace, harmony, joy, goodwill, wisdom, love, truth, and beauty. You are in tune with Universal Mind which knows only wisdom and beauty. *God is a Spirit and they that worship him must worship him in spirit and in truth.* JOHN 4:24.

Life is a state of consciousness. Elevate your consciousness by meditating at every opportunity and carry the realization of it with you into your everyday living. By elevating your consciousness you ensure a life free from tension, worry and emotional conflict.

GOOD LITERATURE HELPS TO EXPAND THE MIND. I am an avid book collector and reader. I have a fondness for browsing in book stores and do it whenever time permits. I am very selective as to the books I purchase. When a book finds a place in my library it gets quite a working over, as I like to underscore paragraphs that present workable ideas or different slants on things.

You cannot go wrong investing in good literature. Books are knowledge and knowledge is power. 'When a man empties his purse into his head, no one can take it away from him', said Benjamin Franklin. Invest your money and time in purchasing and reading *good* books.

THE BEST SELLER OF ALL TIME SHOULD BE IN EVERY HOME. The best selling book of all time is the Bible; a copy of this magnificent book should be in every home and read constantly.

The word 'bible' is derived from the Greek and means 'The Book'. No other book has been read by so many people or been published in so many languages. The Bible presents a true statement of God's will and purpose for man. Its message came out of the subconscious of Prophets. Their wisdom stemmed from the presence and power of God in their lives.

THE GOLDEN RULE IS THE SAME IN ALL HOLY BOOKS. Every religion has its own scriptures on which its faith is founded. Many are considered as the word of God, revealed as revelation, others merely the writings of inspired teachers. Some are clear in their meaning, others are obscure. It is not mere coincidence that the writers of all sacred books have expressed similar ideals. The teaching of the *golden rule* is a case in point. There is little difference in the meaning of the following quotation from the different religions.

CHRISTIANITY:   All things whatsoever you would that men should do to you, do you even so to them.

JUDAISM:   What is hurtful to yourself, do not to your fellow man. That is the whole of the law, the rest is merely a commentary.

BRAHMANISM:   This is the sum of duty: Do naught unto others which would cause you pain, if done unto you.

BUDDHISM:   Hurt not others in ways that you yourself would find hurtful.

CONFUCIANISM:   Do not unto others what you would not have them do unto you.

ISLAM:   No one of you is a believer until he desires for his brother that which he desires for himself.

TAOISM:   Regard your neighbour's gain as your own gain; and your neighbour's loss as your own loss.

The significant message of all sacred books is evident in the golden rule and other similar messages. It is man's relationship with his Creator. This relationship is based on love; love of God and a love of all men and things noble and pure.

Though differently phrased perhaps, there is little difference in the fundamental meanings of many quotations from the sacred books of different religions. Many of the ancient books are surprisingly up to date in their messages. The message of 'love for all humanity', is one that seems to have been pushed aside by modern man and replaced with 'hate and suspicion'. A relationship of love, as expressed in the great books, is the only relationship that will cure the minds of all those intent upon wrong-doing.

If you seek a new lease on life, I urge you to take up reading the most important literary work known—the Bible. Like Prayer, reading the Bible *changes* things.

# SUMMARY OF IDEAS TO ATTAIN
# HAPPINESS AND FULFILMENT

1. *The golden key to successful living is the intelligent application of prayer. Prayer is the mightiest power in the world. When you pray you commune with God.*

2. *PRAYER CHANGES THINGS—Whenever you spend a few quiet moments in prayer, you change both soul and body for the better. God acts for you through your prayers.*

3. *Pray for spiritual and physical strength, for wisdom, joy, happiness. Pray for other people and their good.*

4. *Shoot prayers out at people, especially those who are antagonistic toward you. Shoot out prayers of* **love.**

5. *When you pray, relax, let go. Do not become tense or try to get results by will power.*

6. *Meditation is* **companionship with God.** *When you meditate you experience the presence of God in many ways: joy, peace, beauty, love, wisdom.*

7. *Read the Bible or your chosen Holy Book. Its message is surprisingly up to date. It expresses the wisdom of the ages. It teaches love of God and love of your fellow man, the saving grace of world conflict.*

# HOW TO FORMULATE AN EFFECTIVE SUCCESS PHILOSOPHY

*Success Ideas in this Chapter*

• The Rewards Of An Adequate Philosophy
• Philosophies Of The Great Thinkers Have The Key To Life
• Build A Philosophy On Spiritual Truths
• Love Thyself And Love Others
• Don't Put Others On A Pedestal Or You'll Be Disillusioned
• Plants Thrive On Love
• To Think Evil Of Others Is To Think Evil Of Yourself
• How To Express Love
• When You EXPRESS More You EXPERIENCE More
• Use Past Experience To Mould Your Future
• The Past Is Washed Away By The Tide Of The Future
• Confident Living Is Yours With A Sound Philosophy
• What To Include In Your Personal Philosophy
• Keep On Keeping On
• Summary Of Ideas To Help Form An Effective Personal
  Philosophy

208

# 15

*Philosophy is the art and law of life, and it teaches us what to do in all cases, and, like good marksmen, to hit the white at any distance.*

SENECA

---

**THE REWARDS OF AN ADEQUATE PHILOSOPHY.** Peace and security are not to be found in external things. It matters little how much a man has studied or built up materially, he is not a complete individual until he has perfected his 'inner' self. Material knowledge and possessions do not always bestow happiness and tranquillity. Seldom do they inspire personal integrity. A realization of spiritual truths brings to man contentment and fulfilment.

The aim of every individual should be to develop a practical philosophy of life that will assist in the overcoming of personal difficulties and create a compassionate attitude toward others. To accomplish this aim, discipline of the inner self is required. Thoughts and feelings need to be of the highest order. The rewards for the student of philosophy are many: inner calm, peaceful co-existence with others, physical well-being, happiness and prosperity.

**PHILOSOPHIES OF THE GREAT THINKERS HAVE THE KEY TO LIFE.** Metaphysical training commenced in the oldest of religious systems. Metaphysical schools have continued in India for thousands of years and existed in many of the great nations of the ancient world. The teachings of Plato and Aristotle are still with us, but generally ignored by Western man. The secret of confidence, inner peace and happiness is to be found within the philosophies of the great

209

thinkers of the past; they should be studied by all students seeking success.

The Brahman priests of India, the Buddhist monks of China, Burma and Siam, still practise ancient philosophies handed down through the ages. The purpose of these philosophies is to release the spiritual values in man. Although the teachings are quite simple, their application is difficult and requires a disciplined mind.

BUILD A PHILOSOPHY ON SPIRITUAL TRUTHS. Man's greatest longing is peace of mind. The reason so few achieve a tranquil state of being is because they side-step the spiritual laws to be found in the Bible. Inner peace comes to man when he follows spiritual truths and allows the presence of God to flow through his mind. Dwelling on thoughts of God brings tranquillity of mind and joy.

When you develop a philosophy that is based on spiritual truths, you begin to experience life on a grand scale. When you develop inward perceptions and reach for higher ideals, you become master of your domain.

Begin now, to give thought to the type of person you wish to be and the environment you wish to live within. How do you feel about yourself and your fellow man? What of life itself? Of God? What about your religion? What are your thoughts about its doctrines? Do you believe in life after death? Reincarnation? Look at these things from your *own* point of view, discuss them with a religious practitioner, your family and friends. Read the philosophies of others to enlarge your viewpoint, then formulate a personal philosophy of your own, setting for yourself high standards to live up to. Make sure that your personal philosophy of life is an optimistic one. It should be based on the fact that there is a purpose and definite plan for man. It should have as its premise, a belief in God and His laws. Your life is what *you* make it. An adequate philosophy will provide you with a solid background to achieve happiness and success.

LOVE THYSELF AND LOVE OTHERS. The love of self is necessary in the development of a sound personal philosophy. This does not mean conceit in any form. When an individual recognizes that he is a child of God, he begins to see within himself, things that are worthwhile; the creative things God has blessed him with. One does not condemn God; nor does one condemn that which is *of* God.

If you are 'down' on yourself and hate what you imagine yourself to be, you cannot expect others to like or respect you. *A weak chicken is pecked to death by the strong.* A shy, timid person is a person who is down on himself. He is a person who lacks respect for himself and is the one others tend to 'step on'.

You strengthen your character by respecting your own good. To experience happiness, you have to be able to get along with yourself and your private thoughts. The love of self is first, then you are able to genuinely love others for the good within them. *Thou shalt love thy neighbour as thyself.* LEV. 19:18. Love the worthwhile things within yourself and the worthwhile qualities of others. There is a need within everyone to love and be loved. Others will show love toward you when they see qualities in you that are worthwhile. There is only *one* thing in this life that you owe to your fellow man and that is *love*.

**DON'T PUT OTHERS ON A PEDESTAL OR YOU'LL BE DIS-ILLUSIONED.** To love others is not to put them on a pedestal. Whenever you put someone on a pedestal you'll be disillusioned. The only person to put on a pedestal is God. Some people worship others with greater reverence than they show God. This is a growing trend, particularly among many young people, who reverently worship pop groups, motion picture, television and sports personalities. Show them love as creative individuals of God, as an image in God's image, but do not set them up as human gods. The law of the universe is the law of love. Love your fellow man and love God and you will experience the harmony of life that *is* God. *We know that all things work together for good to them that love God.*—ROM. 8:28.

**PLANTS THRIVE ON LOVE.** An increase in bushels of wheat from a field in Ontario, Canada, which was serenaded with violin sonatas and greater corn yield from a field in Normal, Illinois, over which 'Silver Threads Among the Gold' was played was reported by an associate professor of horticulture at the Ohio Agriculture Experiment Station in Wooster, Ohio.

Experiments by a student at North Olmstead, Ohio, Junior High School used scientific methods to discover the effect of hard or soft words and soft music on plants. Thirteen lima bean plants were subjected to experiments lasting 15 minutes a night for two weeks. The plants were separated into four groups of three each, using one plant as a 'control'.

This 'control' received no stimulus. The other plants were treated variously to Hungarian violin music, to Beatle records, to severe scoldings and to affection. Results showed that the plants which received the affection flourished over the others. The group which was serenaded by violin music grew faster than the Beatle music recipients. And the group which was constantly scolded and accused of being ugly, barely survived.

**TO THINK EVIL OF OTHERS IS TO THINK EVIL OF YOURSELF.** Hate, resentment, ill-feeling toward another human being has no place in your philosophy. To hate another is to hate yourself. To wish evil for another is to decree evil for yourself. We all live within the one Universal Mind. What we think about another, we think about ourselves. If you have an enemy, forgive him now. Let all bitterness and resentment dissolve. You owe your fellow man love; show him love, not hate. Hatred brings high blood pressure and ulcers. Bombard others with thoughts of good, not evil.

Give generously of your understanding and love. Share joy, happiness and prosperity with others. These things return to you in the spirit in which you give them. Show charity and goodwill toward others and it will return to enhance your own life in many wonderful ways.

HOW TO EXPRESS LOVE. An expression of love is one where you attempt to make others truly happy. You always know when you have been successful in your attempt because you experience a good feeling, an 'inner' glow.

Promise yourself that you will make it your business to sincerely express love of your fellow man in thoughts and deeds. Perhaps it might be in the form of inspiration that is offered to another who needs it. It might be in a kindness, a helping hand to a person down and out. When you don't hesitate to express kindness, sympathy, you are expressing love. When you stimulate a desire to express tolerance, kindness, compassion, you are expressing love.

You can make this world a *better* world by expressing a true love of your fellow man. When your heart is filled with love and compassion, you quietly bring about changes in your life. Others will ask the secret of your inner calm and outer show of joy.

Don't put yourself in solitary confinement, bask in the glory of love; love for yourself and for others. To deny love is to deny life itself.

WHEN YOU EXPRESS MORE YOU EXPERIENCE MORE. In order to establish yourself firmly and successfully in life, you will need a philosophy based on *truth* and backed by *faith*. Many times you will be disillusioned, unhappy and frustrated because well-laid plans have gone amiss. This is the time to put your philosophy into play. Know that you are greater than those things that attempt to pull you down. Know that you have the power within to override set-backs, the intelligence to correct your plan of action and the wisdom to know that failure is only a temporary thing. There is a *reason* for every negative situation and event; search for it—a step away, lies the solution.

Life will respond to your new found philosophy when you seek to express more of it each day.

USE PAST EXPERIENCE TO MOULD YOUR FUTURE. The past is 'experience' to be used as a guide to plan the future. To allow yourself to be plagued by negative ideas, false concepts and defeats of the past, is to misinterpret life's plan for you. How could you learn and progress but by trial and error?

Perhaps it would be best to label experience 'learning the facts of life'. Your mind should be 'wide open' and ready to accept new ideas, new concepts. The deeper you delve into philosophy, theology, metaphysics, psychology and psychic phenomena, the faster your fixed notions and false beliefs about life will dissolve. You may not agree with all that you read and hear, but you will see 'another side' and hear strong arguments for and against different points of view that will help you to mould your own philosophy.

**THE PAST IS WASHED AWAY BY THE TIDE OF THE FUTURE.** Life is a school. Many mistakes will be made during the course of your life but the opportunity to profit by them and to make a fresh start is always there. Whatever you may be now, you have not completed your journey. There is 'no end' to the creative road of life other than the end you make for yourself. We all fail ourselves at times, but those who 'rise above' and learn from the experience of defeat, are rewarded.

*The past is washed away by the tide of the future and all that remains is what is God's wish for you.*

**CONFIDENT LIVING IS YOURS WITH A SOUND PHILO-SOPHY.** All it takes to construct a path to confident living is a little courage, a little persistence and a sound philosophy built out of of the wisdom of past experience. Do not be misled by an inadequate philosophy. A sound philosophy offers the opportunity to reshape your life, to add new dimensions of understanding, which brings personal satisfaction, affirmative accomplishment and true happiness. An adequate philosophy elevates your thoughts to the things that are true, beautiful and God-like.

**WHAT TO INCLUDE IN YOUR PERSONAL PHILOSOPHY**

1. TRUTH
2. HONESTY
3. INTEGRITY
4. LOVE
5. LOYALTY
6. WISDOM
7. PEACE
8. COMPASSION
9. TOLERANCE
10. PATIENCE
11. HUMOUR
12. JOY
13. FREEDOM
14. LAWS
15. GOD

**KEEP ON KEEPING ON.** Being happy and successful is not doing what you like in this world but liking what you do. Don't be satisfied with your life as it is, strive to improve it. Put the full force of your creative mind power behind everything you do and set your sights high.

Write off everything of a negative nature that has occurred to you up to now and from this moment on, make your life creative and worthwhile. Have confidence in your abilities. Give yourself free reign to expand and to try *new* things, to meet *fresh* challenges.

Don't attempt to succeed by gritting your teeth and trying to force matters. This is will power and it doesn't work. Look at your plan of action, study the *individual* and *character* motivators you have set for yourself and put them to work. Express yourself through your philosophy and quietly but confidently move ahead, step by step. No one ever climbed a mountain safely and successfully, but by moving slowly, step by step.

Control your emotional problems, not by repressing them, but by *understanding* them. Emotions have no validity unless joined to an idea. Cast aside grievances, annoyances, resentments, worries, jealousies and the like. They stem from negative ideas and create emotional illnesses. When you discharge all negative thoughts about yourself, things and other people, emotional distress is eliminated. You must forgive and forget. Don't say you'll 'forgive but not forget'. Neutralize the toxic poison of hate. Focus on affirmative good.

Don't dwell on the past, or you will induce your mind to produce psychic wounds from your polluted thoughts. When you contaminate your mind with evil thoughts, you contaminate your body and bring about illness. Cleanse the mind. Fill it with thoughts of joy, beauty and harmony. The past is buried in the vacuum of time. Live in the present, within the motion of harmony and believe in what you *can* be. Know that you are fulfilling your creativeness and that you are able to bring forth into your dominion that which you seek. You become happy when you are expressing your true self. Be guided by the truth of God. Know that the wisdom that guides the planets also guides you.

Don't stop with the reading of this book—*go on*. Investigate any and all possibilities that show the way to a better life. Keep off life's treadmill. You have been granted the freedom to choose between being wise or ignorant, healthy or ill, prosperous or poor.

Don't make life awkward for yourself; have the faith of a little child, the wisdom of a great philosopher and the tenacity and strength of a giant. Success is there waiting. You will achieve all that you wish to achieve if you apply the laws of life and *keep on keeping on*.

# SUMMARY OF IDEAS TO HELP
# YOU FORM AN EFFECTIVE
# PERSONAL PHILOSOPHY

1. *The aim of every human being should be to formulate a personal philosophy of life. One that will assist in the fulfilment of goals.*

2. *Build a sound personal philosophy by studying the philosophies of the great thinkers of the past and present.*

3. *Delve into philosophy, theology, metaphysics, psychology and psychic phenomena. Learn all you can about* **life.**

4. *The structure of your philosophy should be based on spiritual truths found in the Bible.*

5. *Set high standards for yourself to live up to. Practise the presence of God in your life.*

6. *Love yourself and your fellow man. All you owe anyone is* **love.** *An expression of love is one which attempts to make others truly happy in an unselfish way. Focus on love, dissolve hate, resentment and hostility.*

7. *Seek to express more and to experience more each day. Develop and use your creative talents.*

8. *The past should only be thought of in terms of 'experience' gained.* **The past is washed away by the tide of the future.**

# CONSTRUCT YOUR
# OWN IMAGE PROFILE

| I AM: | | | I NEED TO BE: |
|---|---|---|---|
| BRASH | | | RESERVED |
| SELFISH | | | GIVING |
| TIMID | | | AGGRESSIVE |
| VAGUE | | | CONCISE |
| INHIBITED | | | FREE |
| INDECISIVE | | | SPONTANEOUS |
| TALK TOO MUCH | | | LISTEN MORE |
| COLD | | | WARM |
| SELF EFFACING | | | CONFIDENT |
| LISTLESS | | | ENERGETIC |
| SELF CONSCIOUS | | | UNAFFECTED BY OTHERS |
| SUSPICIOUS | | | BELIEVING |
| ARTIFICIAL | | | GENUINE |
| TENSE | | | RELAXED |
| PONDEROUS | | | QUICK |
| TOO AGGRESSIVE | | | RESTRAINED |
| BAD TEMPERED | | | HAPPY |
| RUDE | | | CHEERFUL |
| DISHONEST | | | HONEST |
| FEARFUL | | | FAITHFUL |
| TROUBLE MAKER | | | CO-OPERATIVE |

| EXCELLENT: | | | NEEDS IMPROVEMENT: |
|---|---|---|---|
| POSTURE | | | SLUMPING |
| FACIAL EXPRESSION | | | TOO ANIMATED |
| GESTURES | | | EXCESSIVE |
| SPEECH | | | MONOTONOUS |
| DRESS | | | SLOPPY |
| WALK | | | AWKWARD |
| MANNERS | | | IRRITATING |

I consider myself to be:——————————————————

I desire my image to become:————————————————
————————————————————————————
————————————————————————————
————————————————————————————

# How To Succeed Cassette Tapes

## Dynamic Mind Principles That Can Transform Your Life

Learn how to use the amazing powers of your mind to reap a golden harvest of riches, health, and happiness. Don't wait for success — make it happen.

These cassette tapes by Brian Adams, author of the book *How To Succeed,* will help you to achieve your goals and to attain your most secret dreams of success.

Mr. Adams' techniques for personal development are based on years of practical experience — not theory alone. His methods work! His tapes describe the building blocks essential to personal development. And they will teach you how to achieve and to maintain a winning attitude that will serve you in many ways.

Once you feel the success-power within you, your personal and financial goals will become more easily attainable. Brian Adams' techniques will motivate and inspire you in your effort to gain success in any chosen area. You'll be able to direct your energy into creative channels that will produce the positive results you seek.

Mr. Adams' methodology is a breakthough in self-improvement psychology. It will enable you to accomplish the self-motivation and personal growth necessary to reach your goals.

These powerful tapes are offered on a money-back guarantee basis. Listen to the material for just 21 days. Then note the positive dramatic changes that have occurred within yourself.

## How To Succeed Cassette Tapes    $25.00 postpaid

*Send your orders to:*

Melvin Powers
12015 Sherman Road
North Hollywood, California 91605-3781

## Sales Cybernetics Seminars

Brian Adams is available to your organization either as a guest speaker or as a seminar lecturer. Meeting planners: Feel free to call Melvin Powers for complete details.

## Sales Cybernetics

*Sales Cybernetics* is one of the best books ever to be written on the psychology of selling. *Sales Cybernetics* draws its foundation from the "bible" of self-improvement—the classic *Psycho-Cybernetics* by Dr. Maxwell Maltz. This book can open the way to new riches in your life, personally and financially.

320 Pages          $8.00 postpaid

## Sales Cybernetics Cassette Tapes
### The Psychology of Selling

Here's an opportunity to listen to Brian Adams talk about practical selling techniques to increase your income. He will inspire you for your next sale. Listen to these tapes at your leisure as you ride in your car.

Sales Cybernetics Cassette Tapes    $25.00 postpaid

*Please send orders to:*

Melvin Powers
12015 Sherman Road
North Hollywood, California 91605-3781

# MELVIN POWERS SELF-IMPROVEMENT LIBRARY

## ASTROLOGY

| | |
|---|---|
| ____ ASTROLOGY: HOW TO CHART YOUR HOROSCOPE *Max Heindel* | 5.00 |
| ____ ASTROLOGY AND SEXUAL ANALYSIS *Morris C. Goodman* | 5.00 |
| ____ ASTROLOGY AND YOU *Carroll Righter* | 5.00 |
| ____ ASTROLOGY MADE EASY *Astarte* | 5.00 |
| ____ ASTROLOGY, ROMANCE, YOU AND THE STARS *Anthony Norvell* | 5.00 |
| ____ MY WORLD OF ASTROLOGY *Sydney Omarr* | 7.00 |
| ____ THOUGHT DIAL *Sydney Omarr* | 7.00 |
| ____ WHAT THE STARS REVEAL ABOUT THE MEN IN YOUR LIFE *Thelma White* | 3.00 |

## BRIDGE

| | |
|---|---|
| ____ BRIDGE BIDDING MADE EASY *Edwin B. Kantar* | 10.00 |
| ____ BRIDGE CONVENTIONS *Edwin B. Kantar* | 10.00 |
| ____ COMPETITIVE BIDDING IN MODERN BRIDGE *Edgar Kaplan* | 7.00 |
| ____ DEFENSIVE BRIDGE PLAY COMPLETE *Edwin B. Kantar* | 15.00 |
| ____ GAMESMAN BRIDGE—PLAY BETTER WITH KANTAR *Edwin B. Kantar* | 5.00 |
| ____ HOW TO IMPROVE YOUR BRIDGE *Alfred Sheinwold* | 7.00 |
| ____ IMPROVING YOUR BIDDING SKILLS *Edwin B. Kantar* | 7.00 |
| ____ INTRODUCTION TO DECLARER'S PLAY *Edwin B. Kantar* | 7.00 |
| ____ INTRODUCTION TO DEFENDER'S PLAY *Edwin B. Kantar* | 7.00 |
| ____ KANTAR FOR THE DEFENSE *Edwin B. Kantar* | 7.00 |
| ____ KANTAR FOR THE DEFENSE VOLUME 2 *Edwin B. Kantar* | 7.00 |
| ____ TEST YOUR BRIDGE PLAY *Edwin B. Kantar* | 7.00 |
| ____ VOLUME 2—TEST YOUR BRIDGE PLAY *Edwin B. Kantar* | 7.00 |
| ____ WINNING DECLARER PLAY *Dorothy Hayden Truscott* | 7.00 |

## BUSINESS, STUDY & REFERENCE

| | |
|---|---|
| ____ BRAINSTORMING *Charles Clark* | 7.00 |
| ____ CONVERSATION MADE EASY *Elliot Russell* | 5.00 |
| ____ EXAM SECRET *Dennis B. Jackson* | 5.00 |
| ____ FIX-IT BOOK *Arthur Symons* | 2.00 |
| ____ HOW TO DEVELOP A BETTER SPEAKING VOICE *M. Hellier* | 4.00 |
| ____ HOW TO SAVE 50% ON GAS & CAR EXPENSES *Ken Stansbie* | 5.00 |
| ____ HOW TO SELF-PUBLISH YOUR BOOK & MAKE IT A BEST SELLER *Melvin Powers* | 20.00 |
| ____ INCREASE YOUR LEARNING POWER *Geoffrey A. Dudley* | 3.00 |
| ____ PRACTICAL GUIDE TO BETTER CONCENTRATION *Melvin Powers* | 5.00 |
| ____ PRACTICAL GUIDE TO PUBLIC SPEAKING *Maurice Forley* | 5.00 |
| ____ 7 DAYS TO FASTER READING *William S. Schaill* | 5.00 |
| ____ SONGWRITERS' RHYMING DICTIONARY *Jane Shaw Whitfield* | 10.00 |
| ____ SPELLING MADE EASY *Lester D. Basch & Dr. Milton Finkelstein* | 3.00 |
| ____ STUDENT'S GUIDE TO BETTER GRADES *J. A. Rickard* | 3.00 |
| ____ TEST YOURSELF—FIND YOUR HIDDEN TALENT *Jack Shafer* | 3.00 |
| ____ YOUR WILL & WHAT TO DO ABOUT IT *Attorney Samuel G. Kling* | 5.00 |

## CALLIGRAPHY

| | |
|---|---|
| ____ ADVANCED CALLIGRAPHY *Katherine Jeffares* | 7.00 |
| ____ CALLIGRAPHY—THE ART OF BEAUTIFUL WRITING *Katherine Jeffares* | 7.00 |
| ____ CALLIGRAPHY FOR FUN & PROFIT *Anne Leptich & Jacque Evans* | 7.00 |
| ____ CALLIGRAPHY MADE EASY *Tina Serafini* | 7.00 |

## CHESS & CHECKERS

| | |
|---|---|
| ____ BEGINNER'S GUIDE TO WINNING CHESS *Fred Reinfeld* | 5.00 |
| ____ CHESS IN TEN EASY LESSONS *Larry Evans* | 5.00 |
| ____ CHESS MADE EASY *Milton L. Hanauer* | 5.00 |
| ____ CHESS PROBLEMS FOR BEGINNERS *Edited by Fred Reinfeld* | 5.00 |
| ____ CHESS TACTICS FOR BEGINNERS *Edited by Fred Reinfeld* | 5.00 |

_____ HOW TO WIN AT CHECKERS *Fred Reinfeld* ............ 5.00
_____ 1001 BRILLIANT WAYS TO CHECKMATE *Fred Reinfeld* ............ 7.00
_____ 1001 WINNING CHESS SACRIFICES & COMBINATIONS *Fred Reinfeld* ............ 7.00

## COOKERY & HERBS
_____ CULPEPER'S HERBAL REMEDIES *Dr. Nicholas Culpeper* ............ 5.00
_____ FAST GOURMET COOKBOOK *Poppy Cannon* ............ 2.50
_____ HEALING POWER OF HERBS *May Bethel* ............ 5.00
_____ HEALING POWER OF NATURAL FOODS *May Bethel* ............ 5.00
_____ HERBS FOR HEALTH—HOW TO GROW & USE THEM *Louise Evans Doole* ............ 5.00
_____ HOME GARDEN COOKBOOK—DELICIOUS NATURAL FOOD RECIPES *Ken Kraft* ............ 3.00
_____ MEATLESS MEAL GUIDE *Tomi Ryan & James H. Ryan, M.D.* ............ 4.00
_____ VEGETABLE GARDENING FOR BEGINNERS *Hugh Wiberg* ............ 2.00
_____ VEGETABLES FOR TODAY'S GARDENS *R. Milton Carleton* ............ 2.00
_____ VEGETARIAN COOKERY *Janet Walker* ............ 7.00
_____ VEGETARIAN COOKING MADE EASY & DELECTABLE *Veronica Vezza* ............ 3.00
_____ VEGETARIAN DELIGHTS—A HAPPY COOKBOOK FOR HEALTH *K. R. Mehta* ............ 2.00
_____ VEGETARIAN GOURMET COOKBOOK *Joyce McKinnel* ............ 3.00

## GAMBLING & POKER
_____ HOW TO WIN AT DICE GAMES *Skip Frey* ............ 3.00
_____ HOW TO WIN AT POKER *Terence Reese & Anthony T. Watkins* ............ 7.00
_____ WINNING AT CRAPS *Dr. Lloyd T. Commins* ............ 5.00
_____ WINNING AT GIN *Chester Wander & Cy Rice* ............ 3.00
_____ WINNING AT POKER—AN EXPERT'S GUIDE *John Archer* ............ 5.00
_____ WINNING AT 21—AN EXPERT'S GUIDE *John Archer* ............ 7.00
_____ WINNING POKER SYSTEMS *Norman Zadeh* ............ 3.00

## HEALTH
_____ BEE POLLEN *Lynda Lyngheim & Jack Scagnetti* ............ 3.00
_____ COPING WITH ALZHEIMER'S *Rose Oliver, Ph.D. & Francis Bock, Ph.D.* ............ 10.00
_____ DR. LINDNER'S POINT SYSTEM FOOD PROGRAM *Peter G. Lindner, M.D.* ............ 2.00
_____ HELP YOURSELF TO BETTER SIGHT *Margaret Darst Corbett* ............ 7.00
_____ HOW YOU CAN STOP SMOKING PERMANENTLY *Ernest Caldwell* ............ 5.00
_____ MIND OVER PLATTER *Peter G. Lindner, M.D.* ............ 5.00
_____ NATURE'S WAY TO NUTRITION & VIBRANT HEALTH *Robert J. Scrutton* ............ 3.00
_____ NEW CARBOHYDRATE DIET COUNTER *Patti Lopez-Pereira* ............ 2.00
_____ REFLEXOLOGY *Dr. Maybelle Segal* ............ 5.00
_____ REFLEXOLOGY FOR GOOD HEALTH *Anna Kaye & Don C. Matchan* ............ 7.00
_____ 30 DAYS TO BEAUTIFUL LEGS *Dr. Marc Selner* ............ 3.00
_____ YOU CAN LEARN TO RELAX *Dr. Samuel Gutwirth* ............ 3.00

## HOBBIES
_____ BEACHCOMBING FOR BEGINNERS *Norman Hickin* ............ 2.00
_____ BLACKSTONE'S MODERN CARD TRICKS *Harry Blackstone* ............ 5.00
_____ BLACKSTONE'S SECRETS OF MAGIC *Harry Blackstone* ............ 5.00
_____ COIN COLLECTING FOR BEGINNERS *Burton Hobson & Fred Reinfeld* ............ 7.00
_____ ENTERTAINING WITH ESP *Tony 'Doc' Shiels* ............ 2.00
_____ 400 FASCINATING MAGIC TRICKS YOU CAN DO *Howard Thurston* ............ 7.00
_____ HOW I TURN JUNK INTO FUN AND PROFIT *Sari* ............ 3.00
_____ HOW TO WRITE A HIT SONG & SELL IT *Tommy Boyce* ............ 7.00
_____ JUGGLING MADE EASY *Rudolf Dittrich* ............ 3.00
_____ MAGIC FOR ALL AGES *Walter Gibson* ............ 4.00
_____ MAGIC MADE EASY *Byron Wels* ............ 2.00
_____ STAMP COLLECTING FOR BEGINNERS *Burton Hobson* ............ 3.00

## HORSE PLAYER'S WINNING GUIDES
_____ BETTING HORSES TO WIN *Les Conklin* ............ 7.00
_____ ELIMINATE THE LOSERS *Bob McKnight* ............ 5.00
_____ HOW TO PICK WINNING HORSES *Bob McKnight* ............ 5.00

| | | |
|---|---|---|
| \_\_\_ HOW TO WIN AT THE RACES *Sam (The Genius) Lewin* | | 5.00 |
| \_\_\_ HOW YOU CAN BEAT THE RACES *Jack Kavanagh* | | 5.00 |
| \_\_\_ MAKING MONEY AT THE RACES *David Barr* | | 5.00 |
| \_\_\_ PAYDAY AT THE RACES *Les Conklin* | | 5.00 |
| \_\_\_ SMART HANDICAPPING MADE EASY *William Bauman* | | 5.00 |
| \_\_\_ SUCCESS AT THE HARNESS RACES *Barry Meadow* | | 5.00 |

## HUMOR

| | |
|---|---|
| \_\_\_ HOW TO FLATTEN YOUR TUSH *Coach Marge Reardon* | 2.00 |
| \_\_\_ HOW TO MAKE LOVE TO YOURSELF *Ron Stevens & Joy Grdnic* | 3.00 |
| \_\_\_ JOKE TELLER'S HANDBOOK *Bob Orben* | 7.00 |
| \_\_\_ JOKES FOR ALL OCCASIONS *Al Schock* | 5.00 |
| \_\_\_ 2,000 NEW LAUGHS FOR SPEAKERS *Bob Orben* | 7.00 |
| \_\_\_ 2,400 JOKES TO BRIGHTEN YOUR SPEECHES *Robert Orben* | 7.00 |
| \_\_\_ 2,500 JOKES TO START 'EM LAUGHING *Bob Orben* | 7.00 |

## HYPNOTISM

| | |
|---|---|
| \_\_\_ ADVANCED TECHNIQUES OF HYPNOSIS *Melvin Powers* | 3.00 |
| \_\_\_ CHILDBIRTH WITH HYPNOSIS *William S. Kroger, M.D.* | 5.00 |
| \_\_\_ HOW TO SOLVE YOUR SEX PROBLEMS WITH SELF-HYPNOSIS *Frank S. Caprio, M.D.* | 5.00 |
| \_\_\_ HOW TO STOP SMOKING THRU SELF-HYPNOSIS *Leslie M. LeCron* | 3.00 |
| \_\_\_ HOW YOU CAN BOWL BETTER USING SELF-HYPNOSIS *Jack Heise* | 4.00 |
| \_\_\_ HOW YOU CAN PLAY BETTER GOLF USING SELF-HYPNOSIS *Jack Heise* | 3.00 |
| \_\_\_ HYPNOSIS AND SELF-HYPNOSIS *Bernard Hollander, M.D.* | 5.00 |
| \_\_\_ HYPNOTISM *(Originally published in 1893) Carl Sextus* | 5.00 |
| \_\_\_ HYPNOTISM MADE EASY *Dr. Ralph Winn* | 5.00 |
| \_\_\_ HYPNOTISM MADE PRACTICAL *Louis Orton* | 5.00 |
| \_\_\_ HYPNOTISM REVEALED *Melvin Powers* | 3.00 |
| \_\_\_ HYPNOTISM TODAY *Leslie LeCron and Jean Bordeaux, Ph.D.* | 5.00 |
| \_\_\_ MODERN HYPNOSIS *Lesley Kuhn & Salvatore Russo, Ph.D.* | 5.00 |
| \_\_\_ NEW CONCEPTS OF HYPNOSIS *Bernard C. Gindes, M.D.* | 10.00 |
| \_\_\_ NEW SELF-HYPNOSIS *Paul Adams* | 7.00 |
| \_\_\_ POST-HYPNOTIC INSTRUCTIONS—SUGGESTIONS FOR THERAPY *Arnold Furst* | 5.00 |
| \_\_\_ PRACTICAL GUIDE TO SELF-HYPNOSIS *Melvin Powers* | 3.00 |
| \_\_\_ PRACTICAL HYPNOTISM *Philip Magonet, M.D.* | 3.00 |
| \_\_\_ SECRETS OF HYPNOTISM *S. J. Van Pelt, M.D.* | 5.00 |
| \_\_\_ SELF-HYPNOSIS—A CONDITIONED-RESPONSE TECHNIQUE *Laurence Sparks* | 7.00 |
| \_\_\_ SELF-HYPNOSIS—ITS THEORY, TECHNIQUE & APPLICATION *Melvin Powers* | 3.00 |
| \_\_\_ THERAPY THROUGH HYPNOSIS *Edited by Raphael H. Rhodes* | 5.00 |

## JUDAICA

| | |
|---|---|
| \_\_\_ SERVICE OF THE HEART *Evelyn Garfiel, Ph.D.* | 7.00 |
| \_\_\_ STORY OF ISRAEL IN COINS *Jean & Maurice Gould* | 2.00 |
| \_\_\_ STORY OF ISRAEL IN STAMPS *Maxim & Gabriel Shamir* | 1.00 |
| \_\_\_ TONGUE OF THE PROPHETS *Robert St. John* | 7.00 |

## JUST FOR WOMEN

| | |
|---|---|
| \_\_\_ COSMOPOLITAN'S GUIDE TO MARVELOUS MEN Foreword by *Helen Gurley Brown* | 3.00 |
| \_\_\_ COSMOPOLITAN'S HANG-UP HANDBOOK Foreword by *Helen Gurley Brown* | 4.00 |
| \_\_\_ COSMOPOLITAN'S LOVE BOOK—A GUIDE TO ECSTASY IN BED | 7.00 |
| \_\_\_ COSMOPOLITAN'S NEW ETIQUETTE GUIDE Foreword by *Helen Gurley Brown* | 4.00 |
| \_\_\_ I AM A COMPLEAT WOMAN *Doris Hagopian & Karen O'Connor Sweeney* | 3.00 |
| \_\_\_ JUST FOR WOMEN—A GUIDE TO THE FEMALE BODY *Richard E. Sand, M.D.* | 5.00 |
| \_\_\_ NEW APPROACHES TO SEX IN MARRIAGE *John E. Eichenlaub, M.D.* | 3.00 |
| \_\_\_ SEXUALLY ADEQUATE FEMALE *Frank S. Caprio, M.D.* | 3.00 |
| \_\_\_ SEXUALLY FULFILLED WOMAN *Dr. Rachel Copelan* | 5.00 |

## MARRIAGE, SEX & PARENTHOOD

| | |
|---|---:|
| ABILITY TO LOVE *Dr. Allan Fromme* | 7.00 |
| GUIDE TO SUCCESSFUL MARRIAGE *Drs. Albert Ellis & Robert Harper* | 7.00 |
| HOW TO RAISE AN EMOTIONALLY HEALTHY, HAPPY CHILD *Albert Ellis, Ph.D.* | 7.00 |
| PARENT SURVIVAL TRAINING *Marvin Silverman, Ed.D. & David Lustig, Ph.D.* | 10.00 |
| SEX WITHOUT GUILT *Albert Ellis, Ph.D.* | 5.00 |
| SEXUALLY ADEQUATE MALE *Frank S. Caprio, M.D.* | 3.00 |
| SEXUALLY FULFILLED MAN *Dr. Rachel Copelan* | 5.00 |
| STAYING IN LOVE *Dr. Norton F. Kristy* | 7.00 |

## MELVIN POWERS' MAIL ORDER LIBRARY

| | |
|---|---:|
| HOW TO GET RICH IN MAIL ORDER *Melvin Powers* | 20.00 |
| HOW TO WRITE A GOOD ADVERTISEMENT *Victor O. Schwab* | 20.00 |
| MAIL ORDER MADE EASY *J. Frank Brumbaugh* | 20.00 |

## METAPHYSICS & OCCULT

| | |
|---|---:|
| CONCENTRATION—A GUIDE TO MENTAL MASTERY *Mouni Sadhu* | 7.00 |
| EXTRA-TERRESTRIAL INTELLIGENCE—THE FIRST ENCOUNTER | 6.00 |
| FORTUNE TELLING WITH CARDS *P. Foli* | 5.00 |
| HOW TO INTERPRET DREAMS, OMENS & FORTUNE TELLING SIGNS *Gettings* | 5.00 |
| HOW TO UNDERSTAND YOUR DREAMS *Geoffrey A. Dudley* | 5.00 |
| IN DAYS OF GREAT PEACE *Mouni Sadhu* | 3.00 |
| MAGICIAN—HIS TRAINING AND WORK *W. E. Butler* | 5.00 |
| MEDITATION *Mouni Sadhu* | 7.00 |
| MODERN NUMEROLOGY *Morris C. Goodman* | 5.00 |
| NUMEROLOGY—ITS FACTS AND SECRETS *Ariel Yvon Taylor* | 5.00 |
| NUMEROLOGY MADE EASY *W. Mykian* | 5.00 |
| PALMISTRY MADE EASY *Fred Gettings* | 5.00 |
| PALMISTRY MADE PRACTICAL *Elizabeth Daniels Squire* | 7.00 |
| PALMISTRY SECRETS REVEALED *Henry Frith* | 4.00 |
| PROPHECY IN OUR TIME *Martin Ebon* | 2.50 |
| SUPERSTITION—ARE YOU SUPERSTITIOUS? *Eric Maple* | 2.00 |
| TAROT *Mouni Sadhu* | 10.00 |
| TAROT OF THE BOHEMIANS *Papus* | 7.00 |
| WAYS TO SELF-REALIZATION *Mouni Sadhu* | 7.00 |
| WITCHCRAFT, MAGIC & OCCULTISM—A FASCINATING HISTORY *W. B. Crow* | 7.00 |
| WITCHCRAFT—THE SIXTH SENSE *Justine Glass* | 7.00 |

## RECOVERY

| | |
|---|---:|
| KNIGHT IN RUSTY ARMOR *Robert Fisher* | 5.00 |
| KNIGHT IN RUSTY ARMOR *Robert Fisher (Hard cover edition)* | 10.00 |

## SELF-HELP & INSPIRATIONAL

| | |
|---|---:|
| CHARISMA—HOW TO GET "THAT SPECIAL MAGIC" *Marcia Grad* | 7.00 |
| DAILY POWER FOR JOYFUL LIVING *Dr. Donald Curtis* | 7.00 |
| DYNAMIC THINKING *Melvin Powers* | 5.00 |
| GREATEST POWER IN THE UNIVERSE *U. S. Andersen* | 7.00 |
| GROW RICH WHILE YOU SLEEP *Ben Sweetland* | 7.00 |
| GROW RICH WITH YOUR MILLION DOLLAR MIND *Brian Adams* | 7.00 |
| GROWTH THROUGH REASON *Albert Ellis, Ph.D.* | 7.00 |
| GUIDE TO PERSONAL HAPPINESS *Albert Ellis, Ph.D. & Irving Becker, Ed.D.* | 7.00 |
| HANDWRITING ANALYSIS MADE EASY *John Marley* | 7.00 |
| HANDWRITING TELLS *Nadya Olyanova* | 7.00 |
| HOW TO ATTRACT GOOD LUCK *A.H.Z. Carr* | 7.00 |
| HOW TO DEVELOP A WINNING PERSONALITY *Martin Panzer* | 7.00 |
| HOW TO DEVELOP AN EXCEPTIONAL MEMORY *Young & Gibson* | 7.00 |
| HOW TO LIVE WITH A NEUROTIC *Albert Ellis, Ph.D.* | 7.00 |
| HOW TO OVERCOME YOUR FEARS *M. P. Leahy, M.D.* | 3.00 |
| HOW TO SUCCEED *Brian Adams* | 7.00 |
| HUMAN PROBLEMS & HOW TO SOLVE THEM *Dr. Donald Curtis* | 5.00 |
| I CAN *Ben Sweetland* | 7.00 |

| | | |
|---|---|---|
| ___ I WILL *Ben Sweetland* | | 7.00 |
| ___ KNIGHT IN RUSTY ARMOR *Robert Fisher* | | 5.00 |
| ___ KNIGHT IN RUSTY ARMOR *Robert Fisher (Hard cover edition)* | | 10.00 |
| ___ LEFT-HANDED PEOPLE *Michael Barsley* | | 5.00 |
| ___ MAGIC IN YOUR MIND *U.S. Andersen* | | 10.00 |
| ___ MAGIC OF THINKING SUCCESS *Dr. David J. Schwartz* | | 7.00 |
| ___ MAGIC POWER OF YOUR MIND *Walter M. Germain* | | 7.00 |
| ___ MENTAL POWER THROUGH SLEEP SUGGESTION *Melvin Powers* | | 3.00 |
| ___ NEVER UNDERESTIMATE THE SELLING POWER OF A WOMAN *Dottie Walters* | | 7.00 |
| ___ NEW GUIDE TO RATIONAL LIVING *Albert Ellis, Ph.D. & R. Harper, Ph.D.* | | 7.00 |
| ___ PSYCHO-CYBERNETICS *Maxwell Maltz, M.D.* | | 7.00 |
| ___ PSYCHOLOGY OF HANDWRITING *Nadya Olyanova* | | 7.00 |
| ___ SALES CYBERNETICS *Brian Adams* | | 7.00 |
| ___ SCIENCE OF MIND IN DAILY LIVING *Dr. Donald Curtis* | | 7.00 |
| ___ SECRET OF SECRETS *U.S. Andersen* | | 7.00 |
| ___ SECRET POWER OF THE PYRAMIDS *U. S. Andersen* | | 7.00 |
| ___ SELF-THERAPY FOR THE STUTTERER *Malcolm Frazer* | | 3.00 |
| ___ SUCCESS-CYBERNETICS *U. S. Andersen* | | 7.00 |
| ___ 10 DAYS TO A GREAT NEW LIFE *William E. Edwards* | | 3.00 |
| ___ THINK AND GROW RICH *Napoleon Hill* | | 7.00 |
| ___ THREE MAGIC WORDS *U. S. Andersen* | | 7.00 |
| ___ TREASURY OF COMFORT *Edited by Rabbi Sidney Greenberg* | | 10.00 |
| ___ TREASURY OF THE ART OF LIVING *Sidney S. Greenberg* | | 7.00 |
| ___ WHAT YOUR HANDWRITING REVEALS *Albert E. Hughes* | | 4.00 |
| ___ YOUR SUBCONSCIOUS POWER *Charles M. Simmons* | | 7.00 |
| ___ YOUR THOUGHTS CAN CHANGE YOUR LIFE *Dr. Donald Curtis* | | 7.00 |

### SPORTS

| | | |
|---|---|---|
| ___ BICYCLING FOR FUN AND GOOD HEALTH *Kenneth E. Luther* | | 2.00 |
| ___ BILLIARDS—POCKET • CAROM • THREE CUSHION *Clive Cottingham, Jr.* | | 5.00 |
| ___ COMPLETE GUIDE TO FISHING *Vlad Evanoff* | | 2.00 |
| ___ HOW TO IMPROVE YOUR RACQUETBALL *Lubarsky, Kaufman & Scagnetti* | | 5.00 |
| ___ HOW TO WIN AT POCKET BILLIARDS *Edward D. Knuchell* | | 7.00 |
| ___ JOY OF WALKING *Jack Scagnetti* | | 3.00 |
| ___ LEARNING & TEACHING SOCCER SKILLS *Eric Worthington* | | 3.00 |
| ___ MOTORCYCLING FOR BEGINNERS *I.G. Edmonds* | | 3.00 |
| ___ RACQUETBALL FOR WOMEN *Toni Hudson, Jack Scagnetti & Vince Rondone* | | 3.00 |
| ___ RACQUETBALL MADE EASY *Steve Lubarsky, Rod Delson & Jack Scagnetti* | | 5.00 |
| ___ SECRET OF BOWLING STRIKES *Dawson Taylor* | | 5.00 |
| ___ SOCCER—THE GAME & HOW TO PLAY IT *Gary Rosenthal* | | 7.00 |
| ___ STARTING SOCCER *Edward F. Dolan, Jr.* | | 5.00 |

### TENNIS LOVER'S LIBRARY

| | | |
|---|---|---|
| ___ BEGINNER'S GUIDE TO WINNING TENNIS *Helen Hull Jacobs* | | 2.00 |
| ___ HOW TO BEAT BETTER TENNIS PLAYERS *Loring Fiske* | | 4.00 |
| ___ PSYCH YOURSELF TO BETTER TENNIS *Dr. Walter A. Luszki* | | 2.00 |
| ___ TENNIS FOR BEGINNERS *Dr. H. A. Murray* | | 2.00 |
| ___ TENNIS MADE EASY *Joel Brecheen* | | 5.00 |
| ___ WEEKEND TENNIS—HOW TO HAVE FUN & WIN AT THE SAME TIME *Bill Talbert* | | 3.00 |

### WILSHIRE PET LIBRARY

| | | |
|---|---|---|
| ___ DOG TRAINING MADE EASY & FUN *John W. Kellogg* | | 5.00 |
| ___ HOW TO BRING UP YOUR PET DOG *Kurt Unkelbach* | | 2.00 |
| ___ HOW TO RAISE & TRAIN YOUR PUPPY *Jeff Griffen* | | 5.00 |

The books listed above can be obtained from your book dealer or directly from Melvin Powers. When ordering, please remit $2.00 postage for the first book and 50¢ for each additional book.

## Melvin Powers
12015 Sherman Road, No. Hollywood, California 91605

# WILSHIRE HORSE LOVERS' LIBRARY

# Notes